# COOK SMART
# AIR FRYER

# COOK SMART
# AIR FRYER

## 90 quick and easy energy-saving recipes

# DEAN EDWARDS

hamlyn

This book is dedicated to my wonderful parents. Without your life lessons, sacrifice and hard work, none of the amazing opportunities I've had would have even been possible. You have made me the man and father I am today. I love you all.

# CONTENTS

# INTRODUCTION

When did you first jump on the air fryer bandwagon? For a few years now, I've been hearing rumblings about this incredible cooking device that is poised to revolutionize home cooking. But, to be honest, when I first started seeing air fryer recipes pop up in websites, magazines and – of course – on social media, I was slightly sceptical about this method of cooking, and I'm going to explain why. *And* why I was wrong!

I was wrong because – like many people – when I heard the name 'air fryer' I assumed it was a way to fry food with less oil. Which is cool, because it leads to healthier food...but I wasn't sure I would need a whole appliance dedicated to it. My scepticism was blown away when I really started to read up on air fryers: I learned that they are actually mini fan ovens, so anything you can cook in a conventional oven, you can cook in your air fryer at home. I think the name 'air fryer' is a bit misleading: it doesn't do enough justice to what is an absolutely ingenious piece of kit for the home kitchen. Now, I am a total convert.

To give you a little bit of background, I've been an advocate of energy-efficient cookery for many years, first getting interested in – and writing a book about – slow cookers. And, just as with a slow cooker, an air fryer is an incredibly energy-efficient way of cooking. As we all face the rising costs of energy and food, I'm sure I'm not the only one out there who has been looking into reducing my spend, not just through *what* I cook, but *how* I cook as well. At the time of writing, it's much cheaper to run an air fryer for an hour than it is a conventional oven. If you've used one as much as I have, then you will know there aren't many air fryer recipes that require cooking for as long as an hour; in fact, air fryers are so efficient that they cook your meals much more quickly than a conventional oven.

The recipes in this book are designed to be for everyone, even the most novice cooks. I've really tried to use budget-friendly ingredients to keep costs down and I've used simple methods, cutting out any unnecessary steps, to make cooking at home in your air fryer a piece of cake. I want this book to help you to make the most of your air fryer every day. I'm so proud of every single recipe here and I really hope you, your friends and family enjoy them too.

# AIR FRYER TIPS

I tested all the recipes in this book in my dual drawer 7.6-litre (8 quart) air fryer. All were cooked on 'air fryer mode'.

———

I cook many of my recipes directly in the air fryer drawer, both with and without the crisp plate. Air fryers can differ in terms of the model and size, so please adapt my recipes to suit your own air fryer. Some of the dishes will need a suitable heatproof container; the recipes here were tested using a dish measuring 20 × 15 cm (8 × 6 inches). Silicone liners are great if you want to avoid a bit of mess, however please note that they do not conduct heat as well as metal, stoneware or glass, so keep that in mind, as you might need to add more cooking time when you use them.

———

Don't overcrowd the air fryer drawer. An air fryer works so efficiently because powerful fans circulate hot air around the food; the crisp plate needs food to be cooked from all sides.

———

I use a lot of garlic and ginger in my recipes. I recently discovered in my local supermarket jars of minced garlic, minced ginger and a mix of minced garlic and ginger paste. In terms of speed and cost, these are great to use in the recipes in this book. However, if you want to use fresh, then finely grate the equivalent amount (usually in teaspoons) that I use in a recipe.

———

Preheating the air fryer will give you more accurate cooking times. I know the manufacturer's instructions for some models note that it isn't necessary, but I find that getting into the habit of preheating the air fryer gives me great results every time.

———

Because cooking times can be affected by the amount of food in an air fryer drawer, the cooking times in these recipes are always just a guide. You might need to cook a little more or less to get the perfect result. One way I've got around this is to invest in a meat thermometer, or probe thermometer. These are a fantastic way to check if meat or fish is cooked internally to a safe eating temperature. A little bit of knowledge on this subject will go a long way towards boosting your confidence in the kitchen. We always tend to overcompensate with cooking times, to doubly make sure that ingredients such as poultry are fully cooked through, but this often ends up with dry chicken, so trust the science!

—

Because of the powerful fans in the air fryer, sometimes ingredients can become displaced. Toasted sandwiches, in particular, are notorious for the top slice of bread blowing off. Overcome this by securing it with toothpicks, or popping a suitable-sized rack on top.

—

Racks can also be used to allow more food to be cooked within the air fryer drawer, just bear in mind that the top layers of food will brown more quickly than the lower racks, so you might need to rotate them to ensure even cooking.

—

I've tried as much as I can to keep the cooking process for each recipe solely to the air fryer. There are a few occasions where I haven't and my reasoning for this is always that there is a much simpler or more energy-efficient way to do it.

—

# START THE DAY RIGHT

Some say breakfast is the most important meal of the day. I've never really been the sort of person who wakes up hungry – I guess we're all different – so to get my taste buds going in the morning, I have to make sure I'm tucking into something extra-delicious. I do like to mix it up, too, with both sweet and savoury dishes.

But let me tell you this: breakfast has to be easy. So many people skip breakfast because of the bother of making it, but with just a little bit of planning and forward-thinking, you can have a tasty breakfast without much effort.

I can be a creature of habit. When I find something I like, I don't mind eating the same thing every day. My Baked Chocolate Chip Protein Oats are proof of this: I've eaten them every day for a month and I'm still not bored. I just prep enough for three days, pop them into the refrigerator and then bang them in the air fryer every morning for a quick and easy breakfast that keeps me full until lunch.

Breakfast in the air fryer can be so easy – like my Throw-It-All-In Omelette – or fun, like my Fluffy Buttermilk Pancakes that the whole family will love. Knowing what I'm like in the morning, I tend more towards the easier route. Something as simple as bacon cooked until crispy and golden on your air fryer's crisp plate can be ready in mere minutes, but you can also use the bacon fat that drips through to make a crispy fried egg, or you can pop a slice of bread underneath the crisp plate before cooking and let that absorb all the dripping for some no-effort fried bread.

This chapter also includes prep-ahead recipes that are perfect when time is against you and breakfast needs to be portable, such as my delicious On-The-Go Fruity Granola Bars, or my 'boiled' eggs. Yes, you read that right, you can cook boiled eggs in your air fryer.

2 MINS

 8 MINS

 VEGETARIAN

*This is my favourite way to start the morning, and it fills me up until lunch and more. I've recently got back into hitting the gym – not sure how long it will last – but I'm enjoying the routine of going to lift some weights. I try to go early in the morning, then afterwards, as soon as I'm back home, these protein-rich oats kick-start my recovery. Once done, I'm raring to go for the rest of the day.*

# BAKED CHOCOLATE CHIP PROTEIN OATS

**SERVES 2**

80 g (2¾ oz) rolled oats
35 g (1¼ oz) protein powder
1 egg
1 small banana, peeled
   and chopped
120 ml (4 fl oz) milk
1 teaspoon cocoa powder
30 g (1 oz) desiccated
   coconut
½ teaspoon baking powder
a little vegetable oil,
   for the dish
30 g (1 oz) chocolate chips
Lotus Biscoff biscuit spread,
   melted, to serve (optional)

**1.** Preheat the air fryer to 180°C/350°F.

**2.** Blitz all the ingredients, apart from the chocolate chips, in a mini blender or food processor, then pour into a small greased baking dish measuring about 14 × 10 cm (5½ × 4 inches), or two smaller individual dishes.

**3.** Scatter over the chocolate chips, then cook in the air fryer drawer for 8 minutes. I like to finish mine with a drizzle of melted Biscoff spread.

**Tip**

A little protein powder might not be an everyday ingredient, but it's great for keeping you feeling fuller longer, as well as for eating after a workout, to help repair your muscles.

10 MINS

 8 MINS

 VEGETARIAN

*There's something quite magical about the savouriness of a cheesy rarebit topping. Here, it's cooked on top of one of my favourite breakfast go-to ingredients: the humble crumpet. Obviously, this recipe works just as well on toast, but I love the way that the melty filling finds its way into all those beautiful little crumpet holes and, because of this, it's flavour-packed in every single bite.*

# GOOEY RAREBIT CRUMPETS

**MAKES 4**

100 g (3½ oz) mature
    Cheddar cheese, grated
1 teaspoon English mustard
1 tablespoon Worcestershire
    sauce
2 egg yolks
4 crumpets
handful of chives,
    finely chopped

**1.** Preheat the air fryer to 190°C/375°F.

**2.** In a bowl, mix the cheese, mustard, Worcestershire sauce and egg yolks until fully combined.

**3.** Pop the crumpets on the crisp plate in the air fryer drawer and cook for 3 minutes. Remove from the air fryer and spread on the cheese mix, then return to the air fryer for 5 minutes until bubbling and golden.

**4.** Before serving, sprinkle over some chives.

20 MINS

 12 MINS

 VEGETARIAN

*Many years ago, I worked in a pasty shop in Cornwall. I was a student, so it was a bonus that I got to take home leftover food! One of my tasks there was to make scones in the morning – an important job, as Cornish cream teas are famous and scones are the stars of the show. This cheese and jalapeño version is a throwback to that time. The most important thing with these is to eat them while they're fresh; don't let them cool down too much.*

# JALAPEÑO & CHEESE SCONES

**MAKES 6**

---

220 g (7¾ oz) self-raising flour, plus more to dust
½ teaspoon smoked paprika
55 g (2 oz) unsalted butter, chilled and cut into small cubes, plus more to serve
80 g (2¾ oz) Cheddar cheese, grated
1 jalapeño chilli, deseeded and finely chopped
1 egg, lightly beaten
150 ml (5 fl oz) milk, or more if needed
salt

### For the topping
2 tablespoons milk, if needed
20 g (¾ oz) Cheddar cheese, grated

**Tip**

With all scones, it's best to handle the dough as little as possible, for the lightest result.

**1.** Put the flour, paprika and a pinch of salt into a bowl, then add the butter and use your fingertips to rub it in until the mix resembles crumbs. Stir through the cheese and jalapeño, then make a well in the centre. Whisk together the egg and milk, then gradually add this to the well, mixing as you go, until you have a soft but firm dough. Don't be tempted to over-work it, or add more egg mixture than you need.

**2.** Roll the dough out on a floured surface until 2.5 cm (1 inch) thick, then use a 7 cm (2¾ inch) pastry cutter to cut it into rounds. Gently re-roll the trimmings to stamp out more scones and use up all the dough. If you have any egg mixture left, brush it over the scones – or just use the 2 tablespoons milk – then sprinkle over the cheese topping.

**3.** Preheat the air fryer to 200°C/400°F.

**4.** Place the scones on a piece of baking paper in the air fryer drawer, then cook for 12 minutes, or until golden and cooked through. You may need to do this in batches depending on the size of your air fryer.

**5.** Serve warm with extra butter for spreading.

15 MINS

 20 MINS

*I'm pretty sure you get the idea of this recipe from the title of the recipe: as long as you've got eggs in the house, pretty much anything goes. On this occasion, I had peppers and chorizo, Cheddar cheese and a pinch of chilli for a nice kick, but literally add whatever you have going from your refrigerator and store cupboards. It's a great way of using up ingredients that are getting past their best.*

# THROW-IT-ALL-IN OMELETTE

**SERVES 2**

cooking oil spray
6 eggs, lightly beaten
1 green pepper, deseeded
    and finely chopped
½ red onion, finely chopped
40 g (1½ oz) chorizo,
    finely chopped
50 g (1¾ oz) Cheddar
    cheese, grated
pinch of chilli flakes
salt and pepper
wild rocket drizzled with
    olive oil, to serve (optional)

**1.** Preheat the air fryer to 180°C/350°F.

**2.** Spray a heatproof baking dish measuring about 20 × 15 cm (8 × 6 inches) with cooking oil, or use a silicone liner. Decant all the ingredients into the dish, add a pinch of salt and pepper and stir well.

**3.** Cook in the air fryer drawer for 5 minutes, give it a good stir, then return to the air fryer for another 5 minutes, then give it another stir. Return to the air fryer for 10 minutes, or until the eggs are cooked through. Leave to stand for a couple of minutes, to make it easier to remove from the baking dish.

**4.** Serve with some wild rocket drizzled with olive oil, if you like.

0 MINS

 8 MINS

 VEGETARIAN

*This is probably the simplest recipe I've ever written and, yes, sometimes simple is better. Soft-boiled eggs are so tricky to get right... but not any more, with your trusty air fryer! I cook these in bulk for ready-made snacks throughout the week, but, if you want to enjoy them the old-school way, just sit them – still hot from the air fryer – in egg cups, crack the tops off and dip away with some toasted soldiers.*

# SOFT-BOILED EGGS

**SERVES 2**

4 medium-sized eggs,
at room temperature

**1.** Preheat the air fryer to 150°C/300°F.

**2.** Place the eggs gently into the air fryer drawer, cook for 8 minutes, then either place in egg cups and get dipping, or plunge into ice-cold water, peel and enjoy.

### Tips

Take your eggs out of the refrigerator the night before to make sure they are at room temperature before you start to cook.

If batch-cooking your eggs for later, like I like to, once they are cooked, plunge them into ice-cold water. This stops the cooking process *and* makes them easier to peel.

10 MINS

 12 MINS

 VEGETARIAN

*Have you ever eaten a fried egg sandwich? And thought: this is lush, but it's so messy! Well, this ingenious air fryer egg hack is a game-changer. You're basically making a really thin omelette which is attached to two halves of toasted bagel, then, once folded up, it becomes a delicious non-messy breakfast sandwich. I cook mine straight in the nonstick drawer of my dual air fryer, but you can also make this in a suitable-sized baking dish.*

# FOLDED EGGY BAGEL

**SERVES 1**

1 teaspoon butter
1 bagel, halved
cooking oil spray
2 eggs, lightly beaten
1 small tomato, finely
    chopped
1 small bird's eye chilli, finely
    sliced, or ¼ teaspoon
    chilli flakes
30 g (1 oz) Cheddar
    cheese, grated
salt and pepper

**1.** Preheat the air fryer to 190°C/375°F.

**2.** Butter the bagel, then place the halves – cut and buttered sides up – in a heatproof baking dish about 20 × 15 cm (8 × 6 inches). Place the dish in the air fryer drawer, or place the bagels straight into the air fryer drawer. Cook for 4 minutes until toasted.

**3.** Remove the bagel from the air fryer, then either spray the base of your air fryer drawer or your baking dish with oil, pour in the beaten egg and scatter over the tomato, chilli flakes, cheese and a sprinkling of salt and pepper. Place the bagel halves on top of the eggs, cut sides down, then return the dish (if using) to the air fryer.

**4.** Cook for a further 8 minutes, or until the eggs are set, then loosen the egg from the dish or drawer and fold the bagel closed, so the egg is sandwiched in between.

5 MINS

 10 MINS

*Whenever I need a quick breakfast which is filling, tasty and always feels like a bit of a treat, this is the recipe I go to. I love the fact that everything cooks on the bread, so not only do you get a beautifully cooked egg, but you also get toast, tomatoes and bacon, kind of like a light fry-up without the faff. So, my all-important question is: what are you drizzling over the top? Red sauce or brown sauce?*

# BACON & EGG BREAKFAST TOASTS

**SERVES 2**
—

1 teaspoon butter
2 bread slices
2 eggs
4 streaky bacon rashers
8 cherry tomatoes, halved
salt and pepper
ketchup and brown sauce,
   to serve (optional)

**1.** Preheat the air fryer to 170°C/340°F.

—

**2.** Butter the bread, then use the back of a spoon to compress and flatten out the centre part of each slice to create a well. It's important you make this well as large as possible, otherwise the white of the egg will not cook all the way through.

—

**3.** Pop the bread on the crisp plate inside the air fryer drawer, then crack an egg into each well you created. Lay 2 bacon rashers on each slice around the egg, then dot on the cherry tomatoes.

—

**4.** Season with salt and pepper, then cook for 10 minutes.

—

**5.** Serve with ketchup and brown sauce, if liked.

—

10 MINS

 10 MINS

*This is a weekend treat. I'd guess – at one time or another – we've all paid a visit to the golden arches for a takeout breakfast. Now you can make breakfast muffins at home, with the aid of your trusty air fryer. I've added some extra flavourings to my sausage patties, but if you find a sausage flavour combination that you like, then you can use that without the additional ingredients. Why not throw a few hash browns into the air fryer to serve with these?*

# SAUSAGE & CHEESE MUFFINS

**SERVES 4**

4 good-quality sausages, total weight about 300 g (10½ oz)
1 teaspoon dried thyme (optional)
1 teaspoon garlic granules (optional)
4 processed cheese slices
4 muffins, halved and toasted
4 eggs, fried to your liking
ketchup or brown sauce (optional)
pepper

**1.** Skin the sausages and put the meat into a bowl, then add the thyme and garlic granules, if using. Mix well, then shape into 4 patties, each slightly bigger than the muffins. Chill until needed.

**2.** Preheat the air fryer to 200°C/400°F.

**3.** Place the patties on the crisp plate inside the air fryer drawer, then cook for 10 minutes, turning halfway through.

**4.** Place a slice of cheese on the bottom half of a toasted muffin, pop on the sausage patty, then top with a fried egg. Add a little ketchup or brown sauce, if you like, sprinkle with black pepper then top with the other half of the muffin. Repeat to make 4 muffins.

10 MINS

 7 MINS

 VEGETARIAN

*Little ones absolutely love these fluffy pancakes. Chocolate chips are one of my favourite additions, but blueberries are delicious too. I did try to cook these on top of a sheet of baking paper within the air fryer to make cleaning up easier, but I found that the paper kept on moving about so the pancakes didn't come out as round as they should. Saying that, they still tasted lush; looks aren't everything, right? Luckily, my air fryer drawer has a nonstick coating, so I oiled that and cooked the pancakes straight in the drawer. They worked out perfectly.*

# FLUFFY BUTTERMILK PANCAKES

**SERVES 2 / MAKES 6**

90 g (3¼ oz) self-raising flour
½ tsp bicarbonate of soda
40 g (1½ oz) golden
    caster sugar
100 ml (3½ fl oz) buttermilk
1 egg, lightly beaten
30 g (1 oz) chocolate chips
cooking oil spray

**To serve**
1 banana, sliced
maple syrup, for drizzling

**1.** Preheat the air fryer to 170°C/340°F.

**2.** In a large bowl, whisk together all the ingredients apart from the cooking oil spray until fully combined.

**3.** Spray the base of the air fryer drawer with oil, then dot in circles of the pancake mix, around 9 cm (3½ inches) in diameter to make 6 pancakes. You may have to do this in batches depending on the size of your air fryer.

**4.** Cook for 7 minutes.

**5.** Serve scattered with sliced banana and drizzled with maple syrup.

15 MINS

 25 MINS

 VEGETARIAN

*We all know that feeling of dread when you have an early start in the morning. I don't know about you, but I never get a great night's sleep when I know the alarm is going to go off early, so the last thing I want to do is get up and have to make breakfast. Luckily for me, these granola bars are great for this scenario: just pick them up and eat them once you're on the road. Packed with fruit, nuts and oats, they will set you up for the day ahead.*

# ON-THE-GO FRUITY GRANOLA BARS

## MAKES 6

100 g (3½ oz) rolled oats
100 g (3½ oz) mixed nuts, chopped
30 g (1 oz) desiccated coconut
50 g (1¾ oz) pumpkin seeds
50 g (1¾ oz) unsalted butter, melted
50 g (1¾ oz) honey
50 g (1¾ oz) dried cranberries

**1.** Preheat the air fryer to 170°C/340°F.

**2.** Line a heatproof baking dish about 20 × 15 cm (8 × 6 inches) with baking paper, scatter in the oats, nuts, coconut and seeds, then toast for 10 minutes in the air fryer, stirring a couple of times along the way.

**3.** Remove the dish from the air fryer, then stir in the melted butter, honey and cranberries and compress down until flat. Return to the air fryer for 15 minutes to cook until golden.

**4.** Leave to cool in the dish, then remove and cut into 6 equal-sized bars.

# LIGHT LUNCHES

Because of the nature of my work, with lots of very early starts, I do tend to find myself at home at lunchtime, which comes with the benefit of being able to cook myself something tasty to eat. It definitely does have to be something simple to put together though – such as my Cheesy Tex-Mex Turnovers, or Chorizo and Cheddar Tortilla Quiche Bowls – because time is of the essence. After all, like so many of us, I may be at home, but I'm still working.

I also have to think about lunches for my wife Liz. She works long hours, with little chance of stopping for lunch most days, so she needs something to eat at lunchtime that is really accessible and easy.

Because of this, I prep a lot of lunches for her to take to work. For ease, soup is often great for her: she can just pop it in the microwave for a few minutes to warm through before enjoying it with some crusty bread. Now, I know what you're thinking: you can't make soup in an air fryer. Well, I'm here to prove you wrong. You can really intensify the flavour of soup ingredients by cooking them in an air fryer before adding liquid and blitzing into a smooth soup. It's so easy as well. Try my Smoky Mushroom and Paprika Soup, or my Roasted Tomato and Basil Soup. They both really benefit from air fryer cooking. If you want to go the extra mile, dip my Next-Level Cheese and Ham Toastie into one of the soups for the win!

Ultimately, lunch is a pivotal meal. It's important to get some goodness into you at lunchtime to set yourself up for the rest of the day and have a happy, successful afternoon. The recipes in this chapter do exactly that.

15 MINS

 16 MINS

 VEGETARIAN

*This is so fresh-tasting and perfect for making full use of the glut of peppers and tomatoes we have during the summer. I've zapped this up by using one of my favourite condiments – harissa paste – which adds amazing flavour and also a little heat. Bread cubes are a great way to thicken soups. Enjoy this with some crusty bread and butter and, if you like a bit of texture with your soup, try topping with my Crispy Harissa Chickpeas (see page 154).*

# ROASTED RED PEPPER & HARISSA SOUP

**SERVES 2**

2 red peppers, deseeded
    and roughly chopped
200 g (7 oz) tomatoes,
    roughly diced
1 red onion, finely chopped
1 heaped teaspoon
    harissa paste
½ teaspoon ground cumin
1 tablespoon oil
150 g (5½ oz) crustless
    bread, cut into small cubes
200 ml (7 fl oz) boiling
    vegetable stock
salt and pepper
Crispy Harissa Chickpeas
    (optional – see page 154),
    to serve

**1.** Preheat the air fryer to 200°C/400°F.

**2.** Toss the peppers, tomatoes, onion, harissa and cumin into the air fryer drawer, drizzle with the oil, add a pinch of salt and pepper, then mix well. Cook for 8 minutes, then shake well, add the bread cubes and return to the air fryer for a further 8 minutes.

**3.** Transfer everything from the air fryer to a food processer, pour in the boiling stock, then blitz until smooth. Add a splash of water if you prefer a thinner consistency.

**4.** Pour into bowls, season with black pepper and serve topped with Crispy Harissa Chickpeas, if you like.

10 MINS

6 MINS

*Asparagus season is so special to me. Unlike the rest of the year, when we find it in the supermarket at an extortionate price, during the growing season it's so cheap in comparison and it tastes a hundred times better. I just love it simply roasted, as you don't want to mess around with it too much. Simply served on toast with some creamy burrata, this is a brunch dish you will love.*

# ROASTED ASPARAGUS & BURRATA TOASTS

**SERVES 2**

1 bunch of asparagus
1 tablespoon olive oil,
    plus more to serve
1 tablespoon breadcrumbs
4 Parma ham slices
2 sourdough bread
    slices, toasted
1 burrata cheese
finely grated zest
    of ½ lemon
salt and pepper

**1.** Preheat the air fryer to 200°C/400°F. Trim the bases of the asparagus spears by bending them: they will snap at the point where they become tough.

**2.** Toss the asparagus spears in the oil, then season with salt and pepper. Place on the crisp plate inside the air fryer drawer, then sprinkle over the breadcrumbs. Cook for 6 minutes, shaking halfway through.

**3.** Lay the Parma ham on top of the toasts and divide the burrata between them. Top with the asparagus, sprinkle over the lemon zest, season to taste, then drizzle with a little more olive oil to serve.

15 MINS

 20 MINS

 VEGETARIAN

*There are always occasions when you look in the refrigerator drawer and find loads of vegetables just on the turn. What do you do with them? For me, soup is the perfect way to use them up. The vegetables in this creamy cauliflower and parsnip soup are gently spiced, then roasted in the air fryer for extra flavour. I like to serve it with a scattering of croutons on top for texture and a lovely chunk of bread and butter on the side.*

# SPICED CAULIFLOWER & PARSNIP SOUP

## SERVES 2

300 g (10½ oz) cauliflower
    florets
300 g (10½ oz) parsnips,
    cut into chunks
1 onion, roughly chopped
1 teaspoon garlic paste
½ teaspoon ground turmeric
½ teaspoon chilli flakes,
    plus more to serve
1 teaspoon ground cumin
1 tablespoon oil, plus more
    to serve
700 ml (1 ¼ pints) boiling
    vegetable stock
100 ml (3½ fl oz) double
    cream
salt and pepper
croutons, to serve

**1.** Preheat the air fryer to 180°C/350°F.

**2.** Pop the cauliflower florets, parsnips, onion, garlic and spices into the air fryer drawer. Season with salt and pepper, drizzle over the oil and mix well. Cook for 20 minutes, shaking halfway through.

**3.** Transfer the vegetables to a food processor along with the boiling stock and cream, then blitz until smooth. Pour into serving bowls and top with a drizzle of olive oil, some croutons and chilli flakes.

10 MINS

 12 MINS

*Who doesn't love a cheese and ham toastie? You can take this recipe in any direction you want: add pickles, chillies, a beautiful sweet chutney... but one thing I do strongly recommend is that you use mayonnaise instead of butter. This not only crisps up the bread, but adds an extra dimension of flavour. This toastie is delicious served with my Roasted Tomato and Basil Soup (see page 40).*

# NEXT-LEVEL CHEESE & HAM TOASTIE

## SERVES 1

1 heaped tablespoon
    mayonnaise
2 sourdough bread slices
2 ham slices
25 g (1 oz) Cheddar
    cheese, grated
25 g (1 oz) ready-grated
    mozzarella cheese
¼ red onion, finely sliced

**1.** Preheat the air fryer to 180°C/350°F.

**2.** Lightly smear the mayonnaise on one side of each slice of bread. Lay the first slice of bread, mayo side down, on a chopping board. Pop on the ham, then sprinkle on the Cheddar, mozzarella and red onion. Pop the second slice of bread on top, mayo facing out.

**3.** Place the sandwich on the crisp plate inside the air fryer drawer and cook for 12 minutes, turning halfway through.

### Tip

If you are finding that the top slice of bread lifts up in the air fryer while cooking, then pop a couple of cocktail sticks through the sandwich to secure it in place, or rest a wire rack on top.

20 MINS

 14 MINS

 VEGETARIAN

*This rich and creamy soup is a hug in a bowl. I've always found mushrooms a pain to cook in a pan, as they need a high temperature with lots of oil to get the desired caramelization, but not in my air fryer! It's so easy and you will also save on calories from the oil.*

# SMOKY MUSHROOM & PAPRIKA SOUP

## SERVES 2

500 g (1 lb 2 oz) chestnut mushrooms, quartered
1 onion, roughly chopped
1 teaspoon garlic paste
1 heaped teaspoon sweet paprika, plus more to serve
1 teaspoon dried thyme
1 tablespoon oil
200 ml (7 fl oz) boiling vegetable stock
100 ml (3½ fl oz) double cream, plus more to serve
salt and pepper

**1.** Preheat the air fryer to 200°C/400°F.

**2.** Pop the mushrooms, onion, garlic, paprika and thyme into the air fryer drawer, season with salt and pepper, drizzle over the oil and mix well. Cook the mushrooms for 14 minutes, shaking halfway through.

**3.** Transfer the mushrooms to a food processor along with the boiling stock and cream, then blitz until smooth. Pour into serving bowls and top with a drizzle of double cream and some more paprika.

### Tip

It's worth making a larger quantity of soups for quick lunches during the week, as they're easy to transport to the office or eat at home for a couple of days running. Simply dial up the quantities.

20 MINS

 16 MINS

 VEGETARIAN

*Growing up, canned creamy tomato soup was always one of my favourites. This recipe is a nod to that, but I can't lie, it's so much better. Roasting the tomatoes brings out an incredible sweetness that can't be replicated. There's only one thing that can make this even better and that's serving it with my Next-Level Cheese and Ham Toastie (see page 38).*

# ROASTED TOMATO & BASIL SOUP

**SERVES 2**

500 g (1 lb 2 oz) tomatoes
1 red onion, roughly chopped
1 red pepper, deseeded and roughly chopped
2 garlic cloves, roughly chopped
½ teaspoon chilli flakes
1 tablespoon oil
1 tablespoon balsamic vinegar
200 ml (7 fl oz) boiling vegetable stock
100 ml (3½ fl oz) double cream, plus more to serve
handful of basil leaves, plus more to serve
salt and pepper
crusty bread, to serve (optional)

**1.** Preheat the air fryer to 200°C/400°F.

**2.** Put the tomatoes, onion, pepper, garlic and chilli flakes into the air fryer drawer, drizzle with the oil and balsamic vinegar, mix well, then add a good pinch of salt and pepper. Cook for 16 minutes, shaking halfway through.

**3.** Transfer the roasted vegetables into a food processor along with the boiling stock, cream and basil, then blitz until super-smooth. Pour into serving bowls, top with a drizzle of cream, more basil and a scattering of black pepper, and serve with crusty bread, if you like.

10 MINS

 6 MINS

*I'm always up for a bit of a cheat when it comes to quick cooking at lunchtime, so for quite a while I've been using shop-bought Cajun seasoning. If you want to make your own, you can blend the smoky flavours of paprika, cayenne pepper, cumin, dried thyme and oregano together and store it in a jar, but, for time-saving purposes, don't be afraid to grab a version off the shelf and give it a try. These salmon bites are just delicious and the flavours are lifted to a different level with the addition of this sharp and sweet mango salsa.*

# CAJUN SALMON BITES WITH FRESH MANGO SALSA

**SERVES 4**

4 skinless salmon fillets, cut into bite-sized pieces
1 heaped tablespoon Cajun seasoning (see recipe introduction)
1 tablespoon oil
1 tablespoon honey
juice of ½ lime
lime wedges, to serve (optional)

### For the salsa

1 mango, peeled and finely chopped
½ green chilli, finely chopped
½ red onion, finely chopped
handful of coriander leaves
juice of ½ lime
1 tablespoon olive oil

**1.** Combine all the mango salsa ingredients in a bowl and stir well, then leave them to infuse while you cook the salmon.

**2.** Preheat the air fryer to 200°C/400°F.

**3.** Place the salmon pieces in a bowl, add the Cajun seasoning and oil and mix to make sure the fish is coated all over. Cook on the crisp plate inside the air fryer drawer for 6 minutes, turning halfway through.

**4.** Drizzle with the honey and lime juice before serving with the salsa and lime wedges, if you like.

20 MINS

 20 MINS

*My wife Liz enjoys a barbecue base on her pizza instead of the traditional tomato sauce. I'll be honest, I never really appreciated the combination until I developed these Tex-Mex inspired pastries, which are so easy to make and even better to eat. Every single bite has an amazing balance: the sweet, smoky barbecue sauce against the rich salty cheese with a chilli hit... maybe Liz is on to something? One word of warning: please let these cool down before you tuck in. Trust me, I know from experience how hot the filling can be when it's fresh out of the air fryer.*

# CHEESY TEX-MEX TURNOVERS

### SERVES 4

1 sheet shop-bought ready-rolled puff pastry
4 tablespoons barbecue sauce
8 chorizo slices
80 g (2¾ oz) Mexicana cheese, grated
pickled jalapeños, to taste
1 egg, lightly beaten
½ teaspoon dried oregano
cooking oil spray

**1.** Preheat the air fryer to 160°C/325°F.

**2.** Cut the puff pastry into four 12 cm (4½ inch) squares. Smear 1 tablespoon of barbecue sauce diagonally on to each square, add 2 slices of chorizo on top of each line of sauce, then sprinkle the cheese and jalapeños over that.

**3.** Lift up the 2 opposite corners of each square which don't contain the filling. Fold them across the filling so the corners just touch on the top, to form a parcel which is open at both ends. Brush some beaten egg under the point where the pastry corners meet to 'glue' them together, then brush the egg over the rest of the outer pastry. Evenly sprinkle over the dried oregano.

**4.** Spray the crisp plate of the air fryer with oil, then cook the turnovers for 20 minutes.

**5.** Leave to cool for 5 minutes before serving.

15 MINS

 30 MINS

 VEGETARIAN

*You must've been hiding under a rock to have missed out on versions of this dish, which went viral across all social media channels. As soon as I tried this recipe, I knew I was going to cook it for the family for the rest of my days. It's so simple, but ingenious too: the feta, simply baked alongside tomatoes, creates a delicious creamy sauce which literally clings to the pasta. This is definitely one you're going to need to try yourself.*

# ROASTED TOMATO-FETA PASTA

**SERVES 4**

100 g (3½ oz) feta cheese
250 g (9 oz) baby plum
   tomatoes
2 garlic cloves, crushed
   or finely grated
½ teaspoon chilli flakes
1 teaspoon dried oregano
2 tablespoons extra virgin
   olive oil
1 tablespoon honey
320 g (11½ oz) pasta shapes
   (I use casarecce here)
handful of basil leaves,
   shredded
salt and pepper

**1.** Preheat the air fryer to 160°C/325°F.

**2.** Place the feta in the air fryer drawer, then scatter around the tomatoes, garlic, chilli flakes and oregano. Drizzle over the oil and honey, then add a pinch of salt and pepper. Cook for 30 minutes.

**3.** Meanwhile, cook the pasta according to the packet instructions, then drain, making sure to reserve some of the pasta water.

**4.** Stir the tomatoes and feta together and add enough pasta water to loosen it to a sauce consistency. Stir through the basil, then add the sauce to the pasta. Toss until coated, season to taste, then serve.

10 MINS

 25 MINS

 VEGETARIAN

*We always tend to have flour tortillas in the house for times when our daughter Indie is hungry, as they are great for a quick snack to bridge the gap between meals. However, I also love to use them to make these cheat's air fryer quiches. As long as you keep the egg and cream mixture here the same, feel free to experiment with some exciting flavour combinations. I happen to love this smoky chorizo and sharp Cheddar combo.*

# CHORIZO & CHEDDAR TORTILLA QUICHE BOWLS

## SERVES 2

cooking oil spray
2 small flour tortillas
4 eggs, lightly beaten
50 ml (1¾ fl oz) double
  cream
50 g (1¾ oz) chorizo,
  finely chopped
70 g (2½ oz) Cheddar
  cheese, grated
1 tablespoon finely
  chopped chives
wild rocket drizzled with
  olive oil, to serve (optional)
salt and pepper

**1.** Preheat the air fryer to 170°C/340°F.

**2.** Spray a small heatproof bowl with cooking oil. Place a tortilla in the bowl, then place another oiled bowl on top. Cook for 5 minutes. Remove the top bowl. Repeat to crisp up both bowls.

**3.** Beat together the eggs and cream, then season with salt and pepper. Gently stir through the chorizo, cheese and chives, then divide the filling between the crisp tortilla bowls. Cook for 15 minutes, until the filling has set.

**4.** Sprinkle with black pepper and serve with some wild rocket drizzled with olive oil, if you like.

# CRISP IT UP

This is the chapter that you might have been expecting when you first thought about air fryer recipes. An air fryer is an absolutely magical piece of kit for the kitchen: you can use it to cook in so many different ways and the recipes in all the other chapters show you how. But, for many of us, recreating the textures and flavours of fried food without lots of oil is what really draws us towards an air fryer.

To be able to recreate recipes such as Crispy Katsu Chicken, Onion Bhajis or Red Hot Honey Chicken Tender Dogs – without the unhealthiness and calories associated with deep-fried food – is an absolutely amazing bonus of the air fryer method of cooking. When I first got my air fryer, I was actually a little bit sceptical about whether I could cook recipes such as my Roast Crackling Pork or Hot Honey Buffalo Wings without compromising on that crunch you get though conventional roasting or deep-frying, but how wrong I was. I actually think, cooked in the air fryer, they are even better. As an added perk, most of these recipes are ready in far less time than if you were cooking them the old-fashioned, energy-intensive way.

There are some cracking (quite literally) recipes in this chapter that the whole family will enjoy, so why not start to crisp it up?

10 MINS

 12 MINS

 VEGETARIAN

*These are delicious, and my favourite use for them is inside a gyro. I had my first taste of a gyro on holiday many, many years ago and – yes – I'd had a few drinks beforehand. It was bloody lovely. Now I'm seeing really elevated versions of gyros popping up in restaurants and street food stalls all over the place. My favourite includes these crispy halloumi fries alongside the traditional chips, salad and dressings. Load up a warmed flatbread yourself and try it out.*

# CRISPY OREGANO HALLOUMI FRIES

**SERVES 2**

——

225 g (8 oz) block of
    halloumi cheese
40 g (1½ oz) fine dried
    breadcrumbs, or
    panko breadcrumbs
1 teaspoon dried oregano
1 heaped teaspoon
    garlic granules
40 g (1½ oz) plain flour
1 egg, lightly beaten
cooking oil spray

*To serve (optional)*
shredded lettuce
chopped tomato
chopped cucumber
red onion slices
warmed flatbread
tzatziki
chilli sauce
sea salt flakes

**1.** Cut the halloumi into large chip shapes; you should get 16 pieces. Mix together the breadcrumbs, oregano and garlic in a shallow dish, put the flour in another dish and the egg in a third. Coat the halloumi in the flour and gently tap off any excess, then dip into the egg, then finally toss through the breadcrumbs.

——

**2.** Preheat the air fryer to 180°C/350°F.

——

**3.** Place the halloumi fries on the crisp plate inside the air fryer drawer, then spray with oil. Cook for 12 minutes, turning halfway through.

——

**4.** To serve as part of a gyro, load the salad and halloumi fries onto the warmed flatbread, season with salt and serve with tzatziki and chilli sauce.

——

10 MINS

 18 MINS

 VEGETARIAN

*Sometimes you just have to hold your hands up and say: thanks for the inspiration. My good friend the chef James Tanner introduced me to this recipe during a trip to Cornwall. A variation of it can be found on almost every street corner in Mexico. Unfortunately it's tough to get hold of some of their incredible authentic ingredients in the UK, but fear not, my air fryer version is absolutely amazing. Trust me: you will never have sweetcorn any other way again.*

# MEXICAN-STYLE ROASTED STREET CORN

**SERVES 4**

2 tablespoons oil
½ teaspoon smoked paprika, plus more to serve
½ teaspoon ground cumin
1 teaspoon salt
4 sweetcorn cobs
4 tablespoons sweet chilli sauce
80 g (2¾ oz) Parmesan cheese, finely grated
handful of chives, finely chopped
sour cream
lime wedges, to serve

**1.** Preheat the air fryer to 190°C/375°F.

**2.** Mix the oil, spices and salt together in a small bowl, then brush the sweetcorn with it. Place the sweetcorn cobs on the crisp plate inside the air fryer drawer and cook for 18 minutes, turning halfway through.

**3.** Once cooked, brush on the sweet chilli sauce, then sprinkle over the Parmesan and chives. Drizzle with some sour cream sprinkled with extra paprika and serve with lime wedges.

40 MINS

 20 MINS

 VEGETARIAN

*One of my favourite side dishes at my local Indian restaurant is crispy onion bhajis, so I needed to see whether I could recreate them at home in my air fryer. All I can say is: they are a massive success. Gram flour – also known as chickpea flour – can be found in most larger supermarkets now in the UK, on the world foods aisle. Serve these on their own with chutney (my favourites are mango chutney and tomato and chilli chutney), and minted yogurt for dipping, or alongside my delicious Chicken Curry in a Hurry (see page 110).*

# ONION BHAJIS

**MAKES 12**

4 onions, very finely sliced
1 heaped teaspoon salt
   (see tip below)
100 g (3½ oz) gram flour
   (chickpea flour)
½ teaspoon ground cumin
½ teaspoon ground turmeric
½ teaspoon chilli flakes
2 tablespoons finely
   chopped coriander leaves,
   plus more to garnish
cooking oil spray
lime wedges, to garnish
chutney and minted yogurt,
   to serve

**1.** Pop the sliced onions into a bowl, then sprinkle in the salt. Mix well, then leave to stand for 30 minutes, to soften the onions.

**2.** Sift in the gram flour, then add the spices and coriander and just enough water (about 2 tablespoons) to make a thick batter. Mix together gently. Divide the mixture into 12 and shape into patties.

**3.** Preheat the air fryer to 200°C/400°F.

**4.** Spray the crisp plate in the air fryer with oil, then place the bhajis on it. Cook for 20 minutes, turning halfway through.

**5.** Garnish with extra coriander leaves and serve with lime wedges, chutney and minted yogurt.

**Tip**

If you have sea salt flakes, use these to sprinkle over the onions in step 1, as they will soften them without making them taste too salty.

20 MINS

 6 MINS

*Why is it that, so often, the simplest things in life are the greatest? This 6-minute air fryer crispy prawn sandwich – born on the streets of New Orleans in the deep south of America – is truly a thing of beauty. What really sets it off is the remoulade sauce which beautifully complements the sweet prawns. You know by now that I like it spicy, so I splash hot sauce all over mine. This is a must.*

# SHRIMP PO' BOYS

**SERVES 2**

1 tablespoon Cajun
    seasoning
50 g (1¾ oz) plain flour
1 egg, lightly beaten
50 g (1¾ oz) dried
    breadcrumbs,
    ideally panko
200 g (7 oz) raw king prawns
cooking oil spray

*For the remoulade sauce*
3 tablespoons mayonnaise
1 teaspoon Dijon mustard
½ teaspoon smoked paprika
squeeze of lemon juice
hot sauce, to taste
salt and pepper

*To serve*
warmed baguette
shredded lettuce
sliced tomato
lemon wedges

**1.** Preheat the air fryer to 200°C/400°F.

**2.** Mix together the Cajun seasoning and flour in a shallow dish, put the egg in another dish and the breadcrumbs in a third. Coat the prawns in the flour and gently tap off any excess, then dip into the egg, then finally toss through the breadcrumbs.

**3.** Place the prawns on the crisp plate inside the air fryer drawer, spray with oil, then cook for 6 minutes.

**4.** To make the sauce, mix the first 4 ingredients in a bowl, then add salt, pepper and hot sauce to taste.

**5.** Serve the prawns, drizzled in some sauce, in a warmed baguette along with the lettuce and tomato, with extra sauce for drizzling and lemon wedges for squeezing over.

**Tip**

Panko are lightly baked, coarse breadcrumbs, which give all foods coated with them a really shattering crunch. You'll find them in all larger supermarkets.

10 MINS

 15–18 MINS

*Have you discovered hot honey yet? It's honey that has been infused with chilli for a real sweet heat. It works incredibly, not only with chicken, but also vegetables and even cheese (try it drizzled over halloumi, or my Hot Honey Baked Camembert, see page 128). I've listed 'barbecue seasoning or rub' below and you can find something like this in most supermarkets, or venture online for some fantastic companies who specialize in different-flavoured barbecue rubs that are often well worth the investment.*

# HOT HONEY BUFFALO WINGS

**MAKES 12**

12 whole chicken wings, each cut into a drum and a flat
2 tablespoons barbecue seasoning or rub (see recipe introduction)
1 tablespoon oil

**For the blue cheese dip**
100 ml (3½ fl oz) soured cream
50 g (1¾ oz) soft blue cheese
squeeze of lemon juice
small bunch of chives, finely chopped

**For the buffalo glaze**
30 g (1 oz) unsalted butter, melted
2 tablespoons hot honey
50 ml (1¾ fl oz) buffalo sauce

**1.** Preheat the air fryer to 200°C/400°F.

**2.** Dust the wings with the barbecue seasoning or rub, then drizzle with the oil and mix well. Pop them into the air fryer drawer in a single layer and cook for 15–18 minutes, turning halfway through, until cooked through with no trace of pink. If you have a probe thermometer, they should have reached an internal temperature of 75°C (167°F).

**3.** Meanwhile, whisk all the dip ingredients together in a bowl.

**4.** To make the glaze, put the melted butter in a large bowl and stir in the hot honey and buffalo sauce, mixing well. When the chicken wings are cooked, toss them through the glaze, then serve up with the blue cheese dip.

15 MINS

 12 MINS

*One of my favourite memories growing up was a Friday night takeaway. When the choice was ours, my brother Wes and I always opted to share sweet-and-sour crispy chicken balls. Isn't it strange how these food memories stay with us? These are usually served with fried rice but are great with my Salt and Pepper Fries (see page 162).*

# WES'S FAVE SWEET-AND-SOUR CHICKEN

**SERVES 4**

50 g (1¾ oz) plain flour
1 teaspoon salt
1 teaspoon Chinese 5 spice
1 egg, lightly beaten
80 g (2¾ oz) breadcrumbs
   (panko work best here)
2 large skinless chicken
   breasts, cut into
   bite-sized pieces
pepper
spring onions, finely sliced,
   to serve

**For the sweet-and-sour sauce**
2 tablespoons sweet
   chilli sauce
1 small (227 g/8 oz) can
   of pineapple chunks
   in pineapple juice
2 tablespoons cider vinegar
30 g (1 oz) soft brown sugar
4 tablespoons tomato ketchup
1 teaspoon cornflour
50 ml (1¾ fl oz) cold water

**1.** Preheat the air fryer to 180°C/350°F.

**2.** Place the flour in a dish with the salt and 5 spice and grind over a decent amount of pepper. Put the egg in another dish and the breadcrumbs in a third. Toss the chicken through the flavoured flour until coated and gently tap off any excess, then dip into the egg, then finally coat in the breadcrumbs. Place on a rack inside the air fryer drawer, then cook for 12 minutes, turning halfway through.

**3.** Meanwhile, place all the sauce ingredients except the cornflour and water in a saucepan and bring to the boil, then reduce the heat and simmer until the sugar has dissolved. In a cup, mix the cornflour and water until smooth, pour this in and stir well until the sauce has thickened. Keep warm.

**4.** Once the chicken is cooked, place in a bowl, drizzle over the sauce and toss well until glazed. Serve scattered with spring onions.

25 MINS

 1 HOUR 20 MINS

*What's your favourite meat to enjoy for your Sunday roast? I do love a nice rare roast beef, but the crackling on a joint of pork clinches it for me. I have to do everything in my power not to devour it all before it reaches the dinner table. I recommend serving this with my Creamy Leek and Cabbage Gratin (see page 150).*

# ROAST CRACKLING PORK

**SERVES 4**

1 tablespoon oil
1 kg (2 lb 4 oz) pork shoulder joint, skin scored
1 heaped teaspoon sea salt flakes
1 teaspoon fennel seeds

**1.** Preheat the air fryer to 210°C/410°F.

**2.** Rub the oil into the scored pork skin, sprinkle over the salt and fennel seeds then rub those in, too. Place on the crisp plate inside the air fryer drawer, then cook for 15 minutes.

**3.** Reduce the air fryer temperature to 170°C/340°F, then cook for a further hour.

**4.** Finally, crank the air fryer temperature up to its highest – mine goes to 240°C/475°F – then cook for a further 5 minutes. This will help finish the crackling. If you have a probe thermometer, make sure the internal temperature reaches at least 70°C/158°F.

**5.** Rest the meat for at least 20 minutes before carving.

**Tip**

For the perfect crackling joint, leave it uncovered in the refrigerator for 24 hours before cooking.

20 MINS

 38 MINS

*This recipe is perfect if you have a dual drawer air fryer, as you can cook the sauce and chicken at the same time. Don't panic if you haven't though, as you can make the sauce in advance, then reheat it when needed. I'm probably going to get into trouble for making a cheat's version of this famous recipe, so massive disclaimer: this is not authentic in the slightest. But trust me, it's quick, easy and absolutely banging. I like to serve it with some shichimi togarashi (a Japanese spice mixture) for sprinkling on top.*

# CRISPY KATSU CHICKEN

**SERVES 4**

4 skinless, boneless
   chicken thighs
40 g (1½ oz) plain flour
1 teaspoon salt
1 egg, lightly beaten
80 g (2¾ oz) panko
   breadcrumbs
cooking oil spray

*For the katsu curry sauce*
1 carrot, finely chopped
1½ onions, finely chopped
1 teaspoon garlic and
   ginger paste
1 heaped tablespoon
   medium curry powder
1 teaspoon ground turmeric
1 tablespoon oil
4 heaped teaspoons chicken
   gravy granules
250 ml (9 fl oz) boiling water
1 tablespoon honey
1–2 tablespoons soy sauce

*To serve*
steamed basmati rice
shredded white cabbage
sliced spring onions
lemon wedges

**1.** Preheat the air fryer to 180°C/350°F.

**2.** Start with the sauce. Pop the carrot, onion, garlic and ginger paste, spices and oil into the air fryer drawer, or into a suitable container measuring about 20 × 15 cm (8 × 6 inches), then cook for 12 minutes, stirring occasionally.

**3.** In a jug, stir together the gravy granules and boiling water, then add the honey and soy. Pour this over the carrots and onions and cook for a further 10 minutes, stirring halfway through. In a food processor, blitz the sauce until smooth.

**4.** Place the chicken thighs between 2 pieces of clingfilm, then bat down with a rolling pin until they are the same thickness all the way through. Mix the flour and salt on a plate, put the egg onto another plate and the breadcrumbs on a third. Dip the chicken into the flour and gently tap off any excess, then dip into the egg and finally the breadcrumbs.

**5.** Put the chicken on the crisp plate inside the air fryer drawer, spray with oil, then cook for 16 minutes, turning halfway. Make sure the chicken is cooked, with no trace of pink (if you have a probe thermometer, the internal temperature should reach at least 75°C/167°F), then serve on a bed of steamed basmati rice with the hot katsu sauce, shredded cabbage, spring onions and lemon wedges.

15 MINS

 12 MINS

*I just love snacking on tortilla chips, either on their own or – because my favourites are red hot – dipped into a cooling salsa or creamy guacamole. If you don't like the heat, then these crispy chicken tenders can be coated in almost anything: breadcrumbs, your favourite crisps, even crushed-up cornflakes. They can also be eaten on their own with a dip, as well as served in hog dog rolls.*

# RED HOT HONEY CHICKEN TENDER DOGS

**SERVES 4**

60 g (2¼ oz) plain flour
1 heaped teaspoon
    smoked paprika
1 egg, lightly beaten
100 g (3½ oz) red hot tortilla
    chips, crushed (or see
    recipe introduction)
2 skinless chicken breasts,
    sliced lengthways into 4
2 tablespoons honey
2 tablespoons sriracha sauce
salt and pepper

**To serve**
hot dog rolls (I like brioche
    rolls), toasted
coleslaw

**1.** Preheat the air fryer to 190°C/375°F.

**2.** Mix the flour with the paprika and some salt and pepper and place in a dish. Put the egg in another dish and the crushed tortilla chips in a third. Dip the chicken slices into the flour and gently tap off any excess, then dip into the egg, then finally coat well with the crushed tortilla chips.

**3.** Place the chicken on the crisp plate inside the air fryer drawer and cook for 12 minutes, turning halfway through.

**4.** Meanwhile, mix the honey and sriracha sauce in a bowl. When the chicken is ready, toss the crunchy tenders in the sauce until coated. Serve in the toasted hot dog rolls with creamy slaw on top.

40 MINS

 28 MINS

*Yorkshire puddings can be the nemesis of so many cooks, but worry no more. This simple version of classic toad in the hole cooks beautifully in your air fryer. For this recipe, I've used small enamel trays to cook the Yorkshire puddings individually, but if you want to do a larger one and you have the space, you can use a larger circular tray. Great served with mashed potato, cabbage, peas, English mustard and lashings of gravy.*

# PIGS IN BLANKETS IN THE HOLE

## SERVES 2

vegetable oil
4 good-quality sausages
4 smoked streaky
    bacon rashers
½ small onion,
    finely chopped

**For the batter**
80 g (2¾ oz) plain flour
2 eggs, lightly beaten
140 ml (4½ fl oz) milk
½ teaspoon dried thyme
salt and pepper

**Tip**
Place a folded piece of foil underneath your Yorkshire pudding to help you lift it out.

**1.** To make the batter, put the flour in a bowl and make a well in the middle. Pour the eggs into the well, then gradually whisk in the milk until smooth. Add the dried thyme and a good pinch of salt and pepper, then pop in the refrigerator to rest for 30 minutes.

**2.** Preheat the air fryer to 200°C/400°F.

**3.** Either use a large circular heatproof dish, or individual dishes. My individual dishes measure about 18 × 13 cm (7 × 5 inches). Put a good splash of oil into each dish, then transfer to the air fryer drawer and cook for 5 minutes to preheat the oil.

**4.** Meanwhile, wrap each sausage in a bacon rasher. Once the oil is hot, pop 2 into each dish along with the onion and cook for 3 minutes.

**5.** Gently pour in the batter and cook for a further 20 minutes.

# FAMILY DINNERS

My career in food has taken me down so many different avenues, but ultimately my passion lies with family meals, so this chapter is incredibly important to me. The idea of sitting around a table with my family, without any other distractions, means so much to me.

We all lead such busy lives and it can be tough to find the time. But, for me, my memories of growing up enjoying a family meal mean I will always believe it is something I need to make time for – even if it's just 10–15 minutes.

Ultimately, if the food is good, getting everyone around the table is so much easier. And recipes such as my Smoky Chicken Fajitas and Honey & Hot Sauce Baked Ham will always mean the family come running. A lot of the dishes in this chapter can be served family-style, such as the Chicken Shawarma, which can be carved into juicy bite-sized pieces, so everyone can build their own meal with their own choice of favourite breads and toppings. Others are for more special occasions, such as when your child introduces a new partner to the mix, which would be just the right time to serve up Baked Mushroom Wellingtons.

Food is one of the best ways to bring the family together and I hope these recipes will do just that.

15 MINS

 25 MINS

 VEGETARIAN

*The humble cauliflower is a vegetable that has seen an incredible resurgence. Gone are the days when it used to be boiled into a grey mush (sorry, Dad). For me, the best way to cook it is in the air fryer, roasted until beautifully soft on the inside and crispy on the outside. It takes on spices so well, alongside its own earthy flavour. Served simply with this punchy chimichurri sauce, meat-free Mondays will never be the same again.*

# SPICED CAULIFLOWER STEAKS WITH CHIMICHURRI

**SERVES 4**

2 cauliflowers (see tip below)
1 tablespoon Cajun
  seasoning
80 g (2¾ oz) unsalted
  butter, melted
salt and pepper
wild rocket drizzled with
  olive oil, to serve (optional)

**For the chimichurri sauce**
½ red onion, finely chopped
small bunch of coriander,
  finely chopped
small bunch of flat leaf
  parsley, finely chopped
1 garlic clove, crushed
  or finely grated
½ teaspoon chilli flakes
1 teaspoon caster sugar
2 tablespoons red
  wine vinegar
2 tablespoons olive oil

**1.** Put all the sauce ingredients in a bowl. Mix and then season well with salt and pepper. Leave to stand while the cauliflower cooks, to help the flavours develop.

**2.** Preheat the air fryer to 160°C/325°F.

**3.** Cut the cauliflowers into 2.5 cm (1 inch) thick steaks (see tip, below). In a small bowl, mix together the Cajun seasoning, butter and a good pinch of salt and pepper. Brush this on to the cauliflower steaks, making sure you cover both sides.

**4.** Place the cauliflower on the crisp plate inside the air fryer drawer and cook for 25 minutes, turning halfway. (Depending on the size of your air fryer, you may have to cook them in batches.) Serve with the chimichurri sauce and wild rocket drizzled with olive oil, if you like.

**Tip**
Cut the steaks from the middle of the cauliflower; you should get 2 out of each. Use the leftovers for my Spiced Cauliflower and Parsnip Soup, or Cauliflower, Bacon and Blue Cheese Bake (see pages 36 and 164).

10 MINS

 12 MINS

*We've all seen those fajita kits in the supermarket, and with those comes a certain amount of convenience, it's true. But I'm going to show you my way, which is just as easy and – once you invest in the spices – works out a whole lot cheaper. When I cook fajitas, I always ask myself why we don't have them more often. Just load up warmed flour tortillas with the fajita mix, cooling soured cream, salsa and a grating of cheese. A good dash of hot sauce won't go amiss either.*

# SMOKY CHICKEN FAJITAS

**SERVES 4**

2 skinless chicken
   breasts, sliced
100 g (3½ oz) chorizo,
   cut into cubes
1 green pepper, deseeded
   and cut into batons
1 red pepper, deseeded
   and cut into batons
1 red onion, sliced
2 teaspoons smoked paprika
2 teaspoons ground cumin
1 teaspoon dried oregano
2 tablespoons vegetable oil
1 teaspoon salt

*To serve*
warmed flour tortillas
soured cream
grated cheese
tomato salsa
lime wedges

**1.** Preheat the air fryer to 200°C/400°F.

**2.** Combine the chicken, chorizo and vegetables in a bowl, then add the spices, oregano, oil and salt. Mix well until all the ingredients have a coating of spice.

**3.** Decant into the air fryer drawer, then cook for 12 minutes, shaking halfway through.

**4.** Divide among some warmed tortillas, along with soured cream, grated cheese and salsa for loading up and lime wedges for squeezing over.

**5 MINS**

 **25 MINS**

*Chicken thighs have to be one of my favourite things to eat. Not only are they inexpensive, but, when you cook them on the bone, they are always extra-juicy, and – let's be honest – crispy chicken skin is unreal. I just love the sweet-and-sour balance that comes with this sticky marinade. If you are wary of using fish sauce because of its strong aroma, you can substitute soy sauce, but trust me and give it a go, as it adds a delicious umami flavour. Serve with rice and veg on the side.*

# THAI STICKY CHICKEN THIGHS

**SERVES 4**

4 large skin-on bone-in
   chicken thighs
3 tablespoons sweet
   chilli sauce
2 tablespoons sriracha sauce
1 heaped teaspoon garlic
   and ginger paste
2 tablespoons fish sauce
   (or see recipe introduction)
juice of ½ lime
1 tablespoon oil

**To serve**
steamed basmati rice
steamed pak choi

**To garnish**
lime wedges
coriander leaves
chilli flakes

**1.** Preheat the air fryer to 180°C/350°F.

**2.** Put all the ingredients in a bowl and mix well until the chicken is fully coated. Place skin side down on a rack inside your air fryer drawer and cook for 15 minutes. Turn the chicken over and, if you have any marinade left over, use it to baste the thighs.

**3.** Cook for a further 10 minutes, until the chicken is cooked through (pierce the thighs with a knife; the juices should run clear with no sign of pink) and the skin is crispy.

**4.** Serve on a bed of steamed basmati rice with some pak choi and garnish with lime wedges, coriander leaves and chilli flakes.

 1 HOUR 15 MINS, OR OVERNIGHT

 35 MINS

*I love a kebab and, more often than not, I choose chicken over lamb. Spiced and grilled chicken shawarma, which originates in the Middle East, is traditionally served wrapped in flatbread with salad and dressings. It's so easy to recreate at home in your air fryer and you can find shawarma seasoning in most supermarkets, so there's no need to buy all the spices individually.*

# CHICKEN SHAWARMA

**SERVES 4**

500 g (1 lb 2 oz) skinless, boneless chicken thighs
100 g (3½ oz) natural yogurt
1 heaped tablespoon shawarma spice mix
1 teaspoon dried oregano
juice of ½ lemon
1 teaspoon salt

**To serve (optional)**
warmed flatbread
tzatziki
salad
grilled green chillis
chilli sauce

**1.** Place the chicken thighs in a bowl with the yogurt, spice mix, oregano, lemon juice and salt. Stir well, then cover, refrigerate and leave to marinate. Overnight is great, but even 1 hour will do wonders for the flavour. Return the chicken to room temperature before cooking.

**2.** When ready to cook, thread the thighs on to metal skewers. I like to make 1 large shawarma threaded on to 2 parallel skewers.

**3.** Preheat the air fryer to 170°C/340°F.

**4.** Place the chicken skewer(s) on a rack inside your air fryer drawer and cook for 25 minutes.

**5.** Increase the air fryer temperature to 200°/400°F and cook for a further 10 minutes, or until the chicken is cooked. (If you have a probe thermometer, the internal temperature should be at least 75°C/158°F.)

**6.** Serve with warmed flatbread, tzatziki, salad, grilled green chillis and chilli sauce, if you like.

25 MINS

 37 MINS

 VEGETARIAN

*I came up with this recipe because I felt that my vegetarian friends used to get stitched up at Sunday lunch. When we ate out in a restaurant, a veggie roast was basically a roast with the meat removed; no extra effort went into a show-stopper centrepiece for the best meal of the week. But these wellingtons are so good that even those people tucking into the roast beef will feel a little jealous...*

# BAKED MUSHROOM WELLINGTONS

**SERVES 2**

4 large Portobello
 mushrooms
60 g (2¼ oz) panko
 breadcrumbs
½ teaspoon garlic granules
1 teaspoon dried thyme
50 g (1¾ oz) blue cheese,
 crumbled
1 sheet shop-bought
 ready-rolled puff pastry
1 egg, lightly beaten

**1.** Preheat the air fryer to 200°C/400°F.

**2.** Place the mushrooms stalk side down on the crisp plate inside the air fryer drawer, then cook for 12 minutes, turning halfway through. Once cooked, its very important to leave the mushrooms to cool before the next stage. Remove the stalks from the mushrooms and chop the stalks up finely.

**3.** Mix the breadcrumbs with the chopped mushroom stalks, garlic, thyme and blue cheese. Top 2 of the mushrooms with this stuffing in the hollow where the stalks once were, then place the other mushrooms on top, this time hollow sides down, to form 2 parcels.

**4.** Cut two 18 cm (7 inch) squares of puff pastry, place a mushroom parcel on each, then pull in the corners so each mushroom is enclosed in pastry. Turn both over so the seams are underneath, then brush with beaten egg. Poke a hole in the top of the pastry. If you are feeling artistic, score the pastry, starting from the top centre and going down, in curved lines.

**5.** Place on the crisp plate inside the air fryer drawer and cook for 25 minutes until golden.

15 MINS

30–35 MINS

*Hunter's chicken is an absolute pub classic. It works because you have beautiful, juicy chicken, sweet barbecue sauce and rich cheese to give it that luxuriousness. This recipe has been levelled up to include a cheesy sausage stuffing, for that ultimate surprise when you cut into the chicken. I like to eat mine with a little bit more smoky barbecue sauce and serve it up with some crunchy air fryer chips.*

# HUNTER'S CHICKEN PARCELS

**SERVES 4**

2 sausages, skinned
50 g (1¾ oz) Cheddar
    cheese, grated, plus
    60 g (2¼ oz) more
    for the topping
4 skin-on chicken breasts
4 streaky bacon rashers
4 tablespoons
    barbecue sauce

**1.** Pop the sausagemeat into a bowl, add the 50 g (1¾ oz) cheese, then mix well to combine.

**2.** Place the chicken, skin side down, on a chopping board, then gently cut a horizontal pocket into each breast, being careful not to cut all the way through. Place a quarter of the sausage and cheese mix inside each, then close the pockets and turn the breasts skin side up. Fold the thin end of each breast under the main part, then wrap a bacon rasher around to seal the pockets and keep the thin ends in place. Tie with kitchen string to secure.

**3.** Preheat the air fryer to 180°C/350°F.

**4.** Place the chicken, skin side down, on the crisp plate inside the air fryer drawer, then cook for 20 minutes.

**5.** Cut and remove the strings, turn the chicken skin side up and brush on the barbecue sauce and sprinkle over the 60 g (2¼ oz) cheese. Return to the air fryer for 10–15 minutes or until the chicken is cooked with no trace of pink (if you have a probe thermometer, the internal temperature should reach at least 75°C/167°F. Rest for 5 minutes before serving.

10 MINS

 22 MINS

*Pork belly is one of my favourite cuts of meat, not only because it's cheap, but also because of the incredible flavour and richness you get from it. These crispy bites work perfectly with their sweet, sticky and spicy hoisin glaze. Chiu chow chilli oil is a smoky condiment that you can find in the world foods aisle of your local supermarket, but some chilli flakes or sweet chilli sauce will work perfectly, too. I love to eat these with some fluffy rice.*

# STICKY HOISIN PORK BELLY BITES

**SERVES 4**

4 thick-cut pork belly slices
  (total weight about 800 g/
  1 lb 12 oz)
1 tablespoon sesame seeds
4 spring onions, finely sliced

*For the glaze*
3 tablespoons hoisin sauce
1 tablespoon honey
1 teaspoon garlic and
  ginger paste
1 teaspoon *chiu chow*
  chilli oil, or more if
  you like it spicy (or see
  recipe introduction)

**1.** Preheat the air fryer to 180°C/350°F.

**2.** Cut the pork belly slices into bite-sized pieces, then pop them on top of a rack in the air fryer drawer. Cook for 12 minutes, shaking halfway through. Drain off the fat, remove the rack and put the pork belly directly in the drawer.

**3.** Meanwhile, make the glaze by mixing the hoisin in a bowl with the honey, garlic and ginger paste and chilli oil.

**4.** Pour the glaze over the pork belly, then toss well and cook for a further 10 minutes. Once cooked, scatter over the sesame seeds and spring onions and serve.

45 MINS

 1 HOUR 5 MINS

*Christmas wouldn't be the same without a baked ham. In previous years, I've cooked mine the old-school way: gently poached in stock, then roasted in a hot oven. These days, the air fryer makes it much more convenient. For this recipe, I recommend you use a probe thermometer to check the internal temperature of the joint has reached at least 71°C/160°F.*

# HONEY & HOT SAUCE BAKED HAM

**SERVES 4**

1 kg (2 lb 4 oz) boneless, unsmoked gammon joint
handful of cloves

*For the glaze*
50 g (1¾ oz) soft brown sugar
1 heaped teaspoon English mustard
1 tablespoon honey
50 ml (1¾ fl oz) hot sauce

*To serve*
pickled cornichons with onions
English mustard

**1.** Preheat the air fryer to 180°C/350°F.

**2.** Pop the joint on to a work surface and remove the skin. Wrap the whole gammon in foil, then place into the air fryer drawer and cook for 50 minutes, or until cooked through (see recipe introduction).

**3.** Remove the joint from the foil, then score the fat in a diamond pattern. Stud it with a clove in the centre of each diamond.

**4.** Combine all the glaze ingredients in a bowl, then microwave on high for 90 seconds, or until the sugar has dissolved.

**5.** Line the air fryer drawer with foil, pop the gammon back in, then liberally pour the glaze over the ham. Cook for 15 minutes. Rest for 30 minutes before carving.

**6.** Serve with some pickled cornichons with onions and English mustard.

45 MINS

 22 MINS

*You can be as lazy as you want with this recipe and, whichever route you take, it's a real crowd-pleaser. I prefer to make the meatballs myself, adding flavours that I love or just happen to have in the cupboard, but shop-bought meatballs will work just perfectly. This recipe is for 12 meatballs, which can be made ahead of time and frozen for up to 3 months; just make sure they're fully defrosted before cooking. The easy tomato sauce recipe here can be used for lots of other dishes, including as a delicious dip for my Pizza Roll-Ups (see page 103).*

# SPICY MEATBALLS IN TOMATO SAUCE

**SERVES 4**

400 g (14 oz) minced beef
30 g (1 oz) fresh breadcrumbs
1 teaspoon dried oregano
1 teaspoon smoked paprika
½ teaspoon chilli flakes,
    plus more to serve
320 g (11½ oz) spaghetti
salt and pepper
Parmesan cheese, to serve

**For the easy tomato sauce**
1 tablespoon oil
1 small red onion,
    finely chopped
2 garlic cloves, crushed
    or finely grated
400 g (14 oz) can of
    chopped tomatoes
1 heaped teaspoon
    dried oregano
1 tablespoon balsamic
    vinegar

**1.** In a large bowl, mix the minced beef, breadcrumbs, oregano, paprika and chilli flakes with a good pinch of salt and pepper, then combine thoroughly, shape into golf ball-sized spheres and chill in the refrigerator for 30 minutes.

**2.** Preheat the air fryer to 180°C/350°F.

**3.** Add the 1 tablespoon oil for the sauce to the air fryer drawer, then gently place in the meatballs, red onion and garlic and cook for 10 minutes.

**4.** Now increase the air fryer temperature to 200°C/400°F. Give the meatballs a good shake, then pour in the chopped tomatoes, oregano and balsamic vinegar. Cook for a further 12 minutes, gently stirring halfway through.

**5.** Meanwhile, cook the spaghetti according to the packet instructions. Serve with the meatballs and a grating of Parmesan cheese and a sprinkling of chilli flakes.

10 MINS

25 MINS

*These always go down a treat with the family and they're so easy to make. For me, they are quite often a go-to dinner when I can't think what to cook, as I've usually already got the ingredients in. You can find taco seasoning in most supermarkets. I never use a whole sachet, so I save some for the next meal... I knew those old glass spice jars would come in handy at some point. Simply serve these with a crisp side salad for a fantastic family summer meal.*

# TACO STUFFED ROASTED PEPPERS

**SERVES 4**

200 g (7 oz) minced beef
25 g (1 oz) sachet of taco
    seasoning
½ teaspoon chilli flakes
1 small (198 g/7 oz) can
    of sweetcorn
½ pouch (about 125 g/
    4½ oz) of microwave rice
4 large peppers
80 g (2¾ oz) Cheddar
    cheese, grated
1 small (30 g/1 oz) bag of
    tortilla chips, crushed
green salad, to serve

**1.** Preheat the air fryer to 200°C/400°F.

**2.** Place the minced beef in the air fryer drawer, or a suitable heatproof container, then cook for 10 minutes, stirring a few times along the way to break up the minced meat. Add the taco seasoning, chilli flakes, sweetcorn and rice, then stir well to combine.

**3.** Remove the stalk ends from the peppers and take out the cores and seeds. Divide the beef mix between the cavities.

**4.** Reduce the air fryer temperature to 180°C/350°F. Pop the crisp plate in the air fryer drawer, then gently stand the peppers on top and cook for 10 minutes (see tip below). Top with the cheese and tortilla chips, then cook for a further 5 minutes. Serve with green salad.

**Tip**

You may need to cut a bit of the base of the peppers away, to make it easier to stand them up inside the air fryer.

# LIGHTER BITES

This chapter is dedicated to my daughter Indie, who at the time of writing is 13 years old. Indie is the ultimate snacker. No matter how many times I say: 'You're not going to eat your dinner if you tuck into that,' she always manages to finish her food. To be honest, I don't know where she puts it. She must have hollow legs.

Joking aside, though, we all like to turn to lighter recipes when we want something simple and easy within minutes. That could be something just to snack on, but also a full meal when you don't fancy heavy, rich, indulgent food. Some of the air fryer recipes in this chapter – such as the tapas-inspired Gambas Pil Pil with Smoky Chorizo – are great for sharing, if you just want to pick at something.

But lighter recipes must not compromise on flavour. My Miso-Glazed Aubergine, for instance, is an umami-packed show-stopper; there's a reason this dish is a modern classic.

There are several ways to make sure that the food you cook is packed full of punchy flavours. Spice is a great way to ramp up the flavour, so why not try my Chicken Tikka, or my Harissa Roasted Sweet Potato and Couscous Salad, which uses one of my favourite store cupboard ingredients: harissa paste.

10 MINS

 15 MINS

 VEGETARIAN

*This delicious and light summery dish uses one of my all-time favourite ingredients: rose harissa. If you've been following me and my recipes for a while, you will know how much I love the stuff. The spicy North African condiment lives in my refrigerator rent-free and makes weekly appearances in my cooking. It's worth making extra of this recipe for lunch the following day, so don't be afraid to double up the quantities.*

# HARISSA ROASTED SWEET POTATO & COUSCOUS SALAD

## SERVES 2

1 large sweet potato,
    peeled and chopped
    into 2 cm (¾ inch) cubes
1 heaped teaspoon
    rose harissa
½ teaspoon ground cumin
1 tablespoon vegetable oil
150 g (5½ oz) couscous
300 ml (½ pint) boiling
    vegetable stock
80 g (2¾ oz) cherry
    tomatoes, quartered
small bunch of coriander,
    chopped
juice of ½ lemon
1 tablespoon extra virgin
    olive oil
50 g (1¾ oz) feta
    cheese, crumbled
salt and pepper
pomegranate seeds,
    to garnish

**1.** Preheat the air fryer to 190°C/375°F.

**2.** Scatter the potato cubes into the air fryer drawer and mix through the harissa, cumin, vegetable oil and a pinch of salt and pepper. Cook for 15 minutes, shaking occasionally.

**3.** Meanwhile, place the couscous in a bowl and pour over the boiling stock, then cover and leave to stand for 5 minutes. Fork through to separate the grains, then add the tomatoes, coriander, lemon juice, olive oil and feta. Add the sweet potatoes and some salt and pepper to taste, then serve, garnished with pomegranate seeds.

5 MINS

 15 MINS

 VEGETARIAN

*Cooked in any way, aubergines are sponges for flavour. My air fryer version soaks up the flavour of this delicious miso glaze. You can make this vegan, too, by swapping out the honey for maple syrup, or another vegan syrup. Serve with fluffy rice.*

# MISO-GLAZED AUBERGINE

**SERVES 2**
———

1 small aubergine
steamed basmati rice,
   to serve

**For the glaze**
1 teaspoon miso paste
1 tablespoon vegetable oil
1 teaspoon honey
1 tablespoon soy sauce
½ teaspoon chilli flakes

**To garnish**
1 spring onion, finely sliced
toasted sesame seeds

**1.** Halve the aubergine lengthways, then cross-hatch score the flesh deeply on both the cut sides, making sure you don't go through the skin.
———

**2.** Make the miso glaze by mixing the miso paste in a bowl with the oil, honey, soy sauce and chilli flakes.
———

**3.** Preheat the air fryer to 180°C/350°F.
———

**4.** Brush most of the miso glaze on to the cut sides of the aubergine, place the aubergine on the crisp plate in the air fryer drawer and cook for 15 minutes.
———

**5.** Serve the aubergine on a bed of steamed basmati rice and sliced spring onion, drizzled with the remaining glaze and sprinkled with toasted sesame seeds.
———

**Tip**

Miso is one of those ingredients – along with my beloved rose harissa – that can give an instant boost to most savoury dishes, making it truly worth keeping in the store cupboard.

**10 MINS**

 **15 MINS**

 **VEGETARIAN**

*This makes a really cool light lunch. I always keep chickpeas in the cupboard on standby – they are great for making a quick hummus and for adding to curries and stews – but most especially for these fantastic spiced falafels. Falafels are traditionally deep-fried in oil, but you can also do them in the air fryer and, by flattening them, it makes it easier to stuff them into pitta breads.*

# HERBY FALAFEL PITTAS

**SERVES 2**

—

400 g (14 oz) can of
    chickpeas, drained
1 teaspoon garlic paste
1 teaspoon ground cumin
1 teaspoon ground coriander
½ teaspoon chilli powder
3 tablespoons finely
    chopped flat leaf
    parsley leaves
1 tablespoon plain flour
cooking oil spray
salt and pepper

*To serve*
2 pitta breads, toasted
hummus
chilli sauce
salad

**1.** Preheat the air fryer to 210°C/410°F.

—

**2.** Place everything for the falafels except the cooking oil spray into a food processor, then pulse together, seasoning well with salt and pepper. Divide the mixture into 8 golf ball-sized portions, then flatten each slightly.

—

**3.** Place the falafels on the crisp plate inside the air fryer drawer, spray with oil, then cook for 15 minutes until crisp and golden.

—

**4.** Stuff the falafels into warm toasted pittas, with hummus, chilli sauce and salad.

—

5 MINS

 7 MINS

 VEGETARIAN

*The ultimate quick snack for when you are short of time, or when you have friends coming round. Feel free to try different flavours too: Indian-spiced bites are great dipped in sticky mango chutney, or go Italian with dried oregano and garlic to dip away in a rich tomato sauce (for my homemade tomato sauce, see page 86). This combination of flavours is absolutely delicious, especially when the bites are dipped into my Hot Honey Baked Camembert (see page 128). Quick note: make sure to buy unsliced bagels. I learned the hard way...*

# CRISPY BAGEL BITES

**SERVES 4**

2 bagels
2 tablespoons oil
½ teaspoon salt
1 teaspoon smoked paprika
1 heaped teaspoon
   dried thyme

**1.** Preheat the air fryer to 170°C/340°F.

**2.** Cut your bagels into rounds about 5 mm (¼ inch) thick, then place in a bowl. Drizzle over the oil and toss before sprinkling in the salt, paprika and thyme. Mix well to make sure all the bagel slices have some seasoning on them.

**3.** Scatter the bagel slices into the air fryer drawer and cook for 7 minutes, shaking halfway through.

10 MINS

 10 MINS

*If you are craving a taste of Spain, then this garlic-and-chilli prawn recipe spiked with smoky chorizo is perfect for a no-effort air fryer meal. Authentically you'd cook the prawns with the shells on, but if you don't fancy the messy job of peeling them, then of course it's fine to use shelled prawns, as we do here. I do insist, though, on some great bread to mop up all those incredible flavours.*

# GAMBAS PIL PIL WITH SMOKY CHORIZO

**SERVES 2**

50 g (1¾ oz) unsalted butter
40 g (1½ oz) chorizo,
    finely chopped
1 heaped teaspoon
    garlic paste
½ teaspoon smoked paprika
½ teaspoon chilli flakes
200 g (7 oz) shelled
    king prawns
1 tablespoon finely chopped
    flat leaf parsley leaves
squeeze of lemon juice,
    to taste
crusty bread, to serve

**1.** Preheat your air fryer to 200°C/400°F.

**2.** Pop the butter, chorizo, garlic paste, smoked paprika and chilli flakes into a small heatproof baking dish, place in the air fryer drawer, then cook for 5 minutes.

**3.** Once cooked, stir well, then add the prawns and cook for a further 5 minutes.

**4.** Sprinkle in the parsley and squeeze in lemon juice to taste. Serve with crusty bread.

2 HOURS 5 MINS,
OR OVERNIGHT

10 MINS

*This chicken tikka can be used in different ways, such as in a rich curry sauce with some rice, or in a salad, but my favourite way to enjoy it is to load it on to warmed naan with mango chutney, minted yogurt and sliced red onion. It's worth seeking out amchoor (dried mango powder) for this recipe, as it adds a delicious sour citrusy note, though it's still lush without it. You can sometimes buy it from larger supermarkets with a good spice selection, or from subcontinental Asian stores. This tikka also goes great with my Gunpowder Potatoes (see page 160).*

# CHICKEN TIKKA

**SERVES 4**

100 g (3½ oz) natural yogurt
1 tablespoon garam masala
1 heaped teaspoon *amchoor*
   (dried mango powder,
   see recipe introduction)
1 teaspoon ground turmeric
1 teaspoon chilli powder
1 teaspoon salt
1 tablespoon garlic
   and ginger paste
juice of ½ lemon
1 tablespoon mint sauce
3 large skinless chicken
   breasts, cut into
   bite-sized pieces
cooking oil spray

**1.** Mix the yogurt in a large bowl with the spices, salt, garlic and ginger paste, lemon juice and mint sauce. Pop in the chicken and stir well. Cover and refrigerate for at least 2 hours, or overnight if you can for the best results. Return the chicken to room temperature before cooking.

**2.** Preheat the air fryer to 200°C/400°F.

**3.** Place the chicken on the crisp plate inside the air fryer drawer, then spray with a touch of oil and cook for 10 minutes, tossing halfway through, until cooked through. Serve as you like (see recipe introduction for some ideas).

10 MINS

 6–12 MINS

*This is a great way to use up any leftover chicken you may have, dressing it simply in a curried mayonnaise along with some mango chutney for a hint of sweetness. This quesadilla may be different from the classic Mexican dish, but it tastes incredible. I'm using smaller flour tortillas which are perfect for one person. If your air fryer doesn't have space for two quesadillas, cook them one after the other, it doesn't take long.*

# CORONATION CHICKEN QUESADILLAS

**SERVES 2**

200 g (7 oz) shredded
  cooked chicken
3 tablespoons mayonnaise
1 teaspoon mild curry
  powder
2 spring onions, finely sliced
4 small flour tortillas
1 tablespoon mango chutney
100 g (3½ oz) Cheddar
  cheese, grated
salt and pepper

**1.** Preheat the air fryer to 180°C/350°F.

**2.** Mix the chicken, mayonnaise, curry powder and spring onions in a bowl along with a pinch of salt and pepper.

**3.** Take a flour tortilla and spread on a little mango chutney and half the chicken mix. Scatter over half the cheese and top with another flour tortilla. Repeat to make the second quesadilla.

**4.** Cook the quesadillas – one after the other, if your air fryer isn't quite big enough – for 6 minutes, turning halfway through. Cut each quesadilla into quarters before enjoying.

10 MINS

 8 MINS

*Sometimes when you just have to make a snack, you are so hungry that you use whatever you have in the cupboard or the refrigerator. Some great inventions have happened this way, just like the recipe here. These are simply great and, if you want to level them up, then enjoy alongside my tomato sauce (see page 86) as the perfect dipping accompaniment.*

# PIZZA ROLL-UPS

**SERVES 4**

4 white bread slices
1 tablespoon tomato purée
8 pepperoni slices
4 cheese sticks, or 100 g (3½ oz) ready-grated mozzarella cheese
20 g (¾ oz) unsalted butter, melted
1 teaspoon dried oregano

**1.** Preheat the air fryer to 180°C/350°F.

**2.** Slice the crusts from the bread, then use a rolling pin to flatten each slice. Spread on a thin layer of tomato purée, then lay 2 slices of pepperoni on each slice. Add a cheese stick, or divide over the grated mozzarella, then roll up. Brush with the melted butter, then sprinkle with the oregano.

**3.** Pop the roll-ups on the crisp plate inside the air fryer drawer, then cook for 8 minutes.

5 MINS

7 MINS

*These are perfect when you need a quick lunch for the family. I've topped mine with my favourite pizza ingredients, but feel free to use whatever you prefer, or just use the recipe as an excuse to use up some of the ingredients lingering in your refrigerator or store cupboard. I love to use red onion, olives, chorizo and mushroom, but – whatever you do – stay away from the pineapple! You can buy pizza sauce in most supermarkets, but if you can't find it, replace it with tomato passata.*

# CHILLI CHEESE NAAN PIZZAS

**SERVES 2**

4 tablespoons pizza sauce, or tomato passata
2 small garlic naans
80 g (2¾ oz) ready-grated mozzarella cheese
20 mini pepperoni slices
½ red chilli, finely sliced
½ teaspoon dried oregano
wild rocket drizzled with olive oil, to serve (optional)

**1.** Preheat the air fryer to 180°C/350°F.

**2.** Spread the pizza sauce over the naans, then sprinkle with the mozzarella and top with the pepperoni, red chilli and dried oregano.

**3.** Place in the air fryer drawer and cook for 7 minutes until golden and bubbling.

**4.** Serve immediately with some wild rocket drizzled with olive oil, if you like.

2 HOURS

 15 MINS

*Not only is pork shoulder one of the more cost-effective cuts of meat, but it's also one of the tastiest. Traditionally, souvlaki is cooked over the hot coals of a barbecue, but for sheer ease, the air fryer makes light work of this Greek classic. Simply serve with some cooling tzatziki and flatbreads for a real taste of summer.*

# PORK SOUVLAKI WITH TZATZIKI

**SERVES 4**

400 g (14 oz) pork
  shoulder, cubed
1 teaspoon garlic paste
½ teaspoon chilli flakes
1 tablespoon dried oregano
finely grated zest and juice
  of ½ lemon
2 tablespoons olive oil
salt and pepper

*For the tzatziki*
150 g (5½ oz) Greek yogurt
½ cucumber, grated
1 tablespoon mint sauce

*To serve (optional)*
warmed flatbread
Little Gem lettuce
sliced tomato
sliced red onion
chips
lemon wedges

**1.** Put the pork in a bowl with the garlic, chilli flakes, oregano, lemon zest and juice, olive oil and some salt and pepper. If you can, give it a couple of hours, to let the flavours develop. Soak some bamboo skewers in water at the same time. Thread the pork on to the pre-soaked bamboo skewers.

———

**2.** Mix the tzatziki ingredients in a small bowl, then season with salt and pepper.

———

**3.** Preheat the air fryer to 190°C/375°F.

———

**4.** Place the skewers on a rack or crisp plate inside the air fryer drawer and cook for 15 minutes, or until the pork is cooked through, turning halfway through.

———

**5.** Serve with the tzatziki, accompanied by warmed flatbread, lettuce, tomato and red onion slices, chips and lemon wedges for squeezing over.

———

# SAUCE
# IT UP

Welcome to the Sauce It Up chapter. Now, if you've read through the contents list at the start of the book, you may be wondering what this chapter is all about. And, I promise, I thought long and hard about what to call it... but, in essence, the recipes here are all about 'wet cooking' in an air fryer.

When I tell people that you can make classic family-style recipes such as my Spaghetti Bolognese and Chicken Curry in a Hurry in your air fryer drawer, from scratch, they just don't believe me. But I'm here to tell you that this is a fantastic way of utilizing your air fryer to its full potential.

When I was developing these recipes, I took full advantage of the large capacity of my dual air fryer drawers and cooked the vast majority of these saucy recipes straight in the drawer, with the crisp plate removed. But don't panic if you don't have an air fryer model like mine. These recipes, such as my Sausage Casserole, Pad Kra Pao (Pork and Holy Basil), or my Super-Easy Mac and Cheesy can be cooked in a heatproof baking dish in the single drawer air fryer models. For best results, I found a dish measuring about 20 × 15 cm (8 × 6 inches) was ideal, but make sure that any dish you're considering will fit into your air fryer.

Please note, if you are using a silicone liner instead of a heatproof baking dish, you may need to add additional cooking time, because silicone doesn't conduct heat as well as metal or stoneware.

15 MINS

 30 MINS

*This is a bit of a chuck-it-all-in job. Minimal prep work and maximum flavour. I've used a shop-bought curry paste, which you can adjust to your own level of spiciness by adding as much or as little chilli powder as you like. I found the drawer of my dual air fryer was perfect for this curry without the need for a liner, but feel free to use one if you want to save on the washing up. Serve with some fluffy pilau rice and a toasted naan.*

# CHICKEN CURRY IN A HURRY

**SERVES 4**

4 skinless, boneless
   chicken thighs, cut
   into bite-sized pieces
1 onion, finely chopped
1 red pepper, deseeded
   and finely chopped
300 g (10½ oz) can of new
   potatoes, drained and
   cut into bite-sized pieces
1 heaped teaspoon garlic
   and ginger paste
1 teaspoon ground turmeric
½ teaspoon chilli powder
1 tablespoon vegetable oil
400 g (14 oz) can of
   chopped tomatoes
2 tablespoons korma paste
50 g (1¾ oz) natural yogurt
1 teaspoon light brown sugar,
   or any sugar
salt and pepper
coriander leaves, to garnish

**To serve**
pilau rice
toasted naan
mango chutney

**1.** Preheat the air fryer to 200°C/400°F.

**2.** Place the chicken, onion, pepper, potatoes, garlic and ginger paste and spices into a bowl, then add the oil, season with salt and pepper and mix well to coat. Decant the chicken into a heatproof dish measuring about 20 × 15 cm (8 × 6 inches) – or see recipe introduction – and cook for 15 minutes.

**3.** Once cooked, stir, then pour in the tomatoes and curry paste and mix well. Cook for a further 15 minutes, giving it a stir halfway through.

**4.** To finish, stir through the yogurt and sugar. Garnish with coriander leaves and serve with pilau rice, toasted naan and mango chutney.

**Tip**

Shop-bought jars of
ready-made garlic paste,
ginger paste, and garlic
*and* ginger paste, are all
fantastic time-saving
ingredients to have handy
in the refrigerator.

10 MINS

 27 MINS

*The purists will tell you that there's no way you should cook this dish in an air fryer. In truth, this recipe is a million miles away from the traditional Italian slow-cooked ragù, but, when time is of the essence, this version of the classic is absolutely delicious. Serve up with a grating of cheese and maybe some garlic bread on the side. I promise you, not a single person will complain. It's absolutely lush.*

# SPAGHETTI BOLOGNESE

**SERVES 4**

400 g (14 oz) minced beef
1 small onion, finely chopped
1 small carrot, very
   finely chopped
1 teaspoon garlic paste
½ teaspoon chilli flakes
1 heaped teaspoon
   dried oregano
150 ml (¼ pint) boiling
   beef stock
400 g (14 oz) can of
   chopped tomatoes
320 g (11½ oz) spaghetti
salt and pepper

***To garnish***
basil leaves
grated Parmesan cheese

**1.** Preheat the air fryer to 200°C/400°F.

**2.** Put the minced meat directly into the air fryer drawer, or into a heatproof container measuring about 20 × 15 cm (8 × 6 inches). Add the onion, carrot and a pinch of salt and pepper and cook for 12 minutes, stirring twice during the cooking process to break up the minced meat.

**3.** Add the garlic, chilli flakes and dried oregano, then pour in the stock and tomatoes and stir well. Cook for a further 15 minutes.

**4.** Meanwhile, cook the pasta according to the packet instructions, then serve with the sauce, scattered with basil leaves and grated Parmesan.

15 MINS

 16 MINS

 VEGETARIAN

*Can you believe this incredible mac and cheese contains only five ingredients? Well, four really, but I'm counting the two different types of cheese as individual ingredients. My daughter Indie is an absolute super-fan of mac and cheese, and this air fryer version is so simple to knock up. So if your kids love to moan when they're hungry, like mine does, this is a recipe that can be on the table in minutes.*

# SUPER-EASY MAC & CHEESY

### SERVES 2

200 g (7 oz) macaroni pasta
410 g (14½ oz) can of evaporated milk
60 g (2¼ oz) Cheddar cheese, grated, plus more for topping
60 g (2¼ oz) ready-grated mozzarella cheese, plus more for topping
handful of chives, chopped, to serve

**1.** Preheat the air fryer to 180°C/350°F.

**2.** Cook the pasta according to the packet instructions, then transfer to a silicone liner or a heatproof baking dish measuring about 20 × 15 cm (8 × 6 inches). Pour in the evaporated milk, add both cheeses, then stir together.

**3.** Cook in the air fryer drawer for 16 minutes. Halfway through, give it a stir, then top with a little more of both types of cheese. Leave to cool for a couple of minutes, then sprinkle over the chives to serve.

15 MINS

 27 MINS

 VEGETARIAN

*Ratatouille is a classic French dish, packed full of incredible flavours. What I love about this recipe is that the air fryer creates an amazing flavour profile by just roasting the vegetables until they become almost sweet and caramelized. Rather than treating this as a side dish, adding a can of chopped tomatoes turns it into an incredible sauce for pasta. Once cooked, just toss your pasta through. Bloody lovely.*

# RATATOUILLE PASTA

**SERVES 4**

1 small aubergine, cut into 1 cm (½ inch) chunks
1 red pepper, deseeded and cut into 1 cm (½ inch) chunks
1 courgette, cut into 1 cm (½ inch) chunks
1 red onion, cut into 1 cm (½ inch) chunks
1 heaped teaspoon garlic paste
1 teaspoon dried thyme
2 tablespoons olive oil
400 g (14 oz) can of chopped tomatoes
240 g (8½ oz) pasta of your choice
salt and pepper
basil leaves, to serve

**1.** Preheat the air fryer to 200°C/400°F.

**2.** Pop the aubergine, pepper, courgette, onion, garlic paste, thyme and a pinch of salt and pepper into a bowl, drizzle with the oil and toss well until coated.

**3.** Tip the vegetables into the air fryer drawer, or a heatproof container measuring about 20 × 15 cm (8 × 6 inches), then cook for 12 minutes, stirring halfway through.

**4.** Pour in the tomatoes, then cook for a further 15 minutes, stirring halfway through.

**5.** Meanwhile cook the pasta according to the packet instructions, then drain. Toss the pasta with the ratatouille, then serve, scattered with torn basil leaves.

10 MINS

 18 MINS

*I was lucky enough to be cooked this incredible Thai dish by my friend Sasiphim, who is an amazing chef in her own right. I won't lie: the amount of chilli in her dish knocked my socks off, but I could not stop eating it. And, to this day, I don't think I've ever eaten anything better, it was that delicious. Now here is my disclaimer: sorry, Sasiphim, this is in no way as authentic a recipe as yours, but I had to attempt my own home-cooked air fryer version. Serve with some jasmine rice, and a fried egg is a lush addition.*

# PAD KRA PAO PORK & HOLY BASIL

**SERVES 4**

400 g (14 oz) minced pork
1 small onion, finely chopped
1 heaped teaspoon
    garlic paste
4 Thai chillies, finely
    sliced (see tip below)
1 heaped teaspoon
    caster sugar
1 tablespoon fish sauce
2 tablespoons oyster sauce
handful of holy basil leaves
    (or substitute with Thai
    or Italian basil)

***To serve***
jasmine rice
4 fried eggs (optional)

**1.** Preheat your air fryer to 200°C/400°F.

**2.** Put the minced pork into a heatproof container measuring about 20 × 15 cm (8 × 6 inches). Add the onion, garlic paste and chillies, pop it into the air fryer drawer and cook for 12 minutes, stirring twice during the cooking process to break up the minced meat.

**3.** Stir through the sugar, fish sauce and oyster sauce, then cook for a further 6 minutes.

**4.** Finally, stir through the holy basil until wilted, then serve with jasmine rice, and top with fried eggs, if you like.

**Tip**

Yes, 4 Thai chillies is a lot of heat, but authentically this dish is even hotter than that, so if you can, be brave and try it with the full amount.

**10 MINS**

 **27 MINS**

*I love the memories that a good old sausage casserole brings back for me. My mum used to make it for us as kids, cooked for so long that the sausages nearly fell apart. It was so good. This economical recipe hits the mark, just like mum's did, especially when you serve it with creamy mashed potato to soak up all that gravy. I actually cook the casserole straight inside my dual air fryer drawer, but you can also cook it inside a heatproof container.*

# SAUSAGE CASSEROLE

**SERVES 4**
———

8 good-quality pork
   sausages (I like pork
   and apple)
1 onion, finely chopped
1 red pepper, deseeded
   and finely chopped
1 tablespoon oil
4 heaped teaspoons
   chicken gravy granules
200 ml (7 fl oz) boiling water
200 ml (7 fl oz) dry cider,
   or boiling vegetable stock
1 teaspoon dried thyme
1 teaspoon wholegrain
   mustard
salt and pepper

*To serve*
creamy mashed potato
steamed spinach

**1.** Preheat the air fryer to 200°C/400°F.
———

**2.** Throw the sausages, onion and pepper into a heatproof container measuring about 20 × 18 cm (8 × 6 inches). Add the oil, shake well, then cook for 12 minutes, shaking halfway through.
———

**3.** Meanwhile, mix the gravy granules with the boiling water, stir well, then add the cider or stock, thyme and mustard with a pinch of salt and pepper and stir well again.
———

**4.** Reduce the air fryer temperature to 180°C/350°F. Pour the gravy in with the sausages, stir well, then cook for a further 15 minutes, stirring occasionally.
———

**5.** Serve with creamy mashed potato and steamed spinach.
———

15 MINS

 12 MINS

*I'm going to take you back to a time when I was a skint student, money was of the essence and any budget for luxurious food was an absolute fantasy. This beauty of a recipe was dreamed up out of the stuff that I had in the cupboard at the time... and, you know what? I loved it. To this day I still cook this dish and it always reminds me of the good times. It's hearty and tasty and also easy on the wallet. Of course, if your air fryer is big enough, you could double up this recipe and cook it for four.*

# TUNA PASTA BAKE

**SERVES 2**

120 g (4¼ oz) cooked
    pasta shapes
400 g (14 oz) can
    of chicken soup
145 g (5¼ oz) can
    of tuna, drained
200 g (7 oz) can of
    sweetcorn, drained
100 g (3½ oz) Cheddar
    cheese, grated
30 g (1 oz) packet of
    salt and vinegar
    crisps, crushed

**1.** Preheat the air fryer to 200°C/400°F.

**2.** Put the cooked, drained pasta into a bowl, then pour in the soup. Stir through the tuna and sweetcorn until fully combined, then pour into your air fryer drawer, or decant into a suitable-sized baking dish measuring about 20 × 15 cm (8 × 6 inches) and place in the air fryer drawer. Scatter over the cheese and cook for 12 minutes.

**3.** Once cooked, crumble over the crisps, then serve.

10 MINS

37 MINS

*Do you ever eat something and automatically it just conjures up memories from childhood? My lovely mother-in-law Vicky is a fantastic cook. That talent might have skipped a generation with my wife Liz, but it's always nice to be cooked for. One day we were there for dinner and Vicky cooked us an incredible chicken and broccoli bake, creamy, rich and delicious. So I had to put my own air fryer spin on it.*

# OUR VIC'S CHICKEN & BROCCOLI BAKE

**SERVES 2**

250 g (9 oz) skinless, boneless chicken thighs, roughly chopped
small head of broccoli, cut into florets
½ teaspoon garlic paste
½ teaspoon dried thyme
splash of oil
60 g (2¼ oz) cream cheese
400 g (14 oz) can of chicken and mushroom soup
30 g (1 oz) fresh breadcrumbs
30 g (1 oz) Parmesan cheese, finely grated
salt and pepper

**1.** Preheat the air fryer to 180°C/350°F.

**2.** Place the chicken, broccoli, garlic paste and thyme in a bowl, then add the splash of oil, season with salt and pepper and mix well to coat.

**3.** Tip into a heatproof dish or silicone liner measuring about 20 × 15 cm (8 × 6 inches), pop it into your air fryer drawer and cook for 12 minutes, stirring a couple of times along the way.

**4.** Stir through the cream cheese and soup, then top with the breadcrumbs and Parmesan. Return to the air fryer for 25 minutes, or until golden and bubbling.

10 MINS

 17 MINS

*Using minced meat in recipes definitely makes the meal both more economical and seem to go that much further. I always love it when you can create a whole recipe in the air fryer drawer and this is both simple and delicious to put together. I serve this with egg noodles, which get tossed through the sauce at the last minute along with a sprinkling of spring onion for colour and crunch.*

# PORK & BLACK BEAN NOODLES

**SERVES 4**

400 g (14 oz) minced pork
1 onion, finely chopped
1 heaped teaspoon ginger
    and garlic paste
1 green pepper, deseeded
    and finely chopped
2 tablespoons black
    bean paste
1 tablespoon soy sauce
100 ml (3½ fl oz) boiling
    beef stock
1 tablespoon honey
salt and pepper

**To serve**
200g (7 oz) egg noodles
    (about 4 'nests')
4 spring onions, finely sliced

**1.** Preheat the air fryer to 200°C/400°F.

**2.** Put the minced pork into a heatproof baking dish measuring about 20 × 15 cm (8 × 6 inches), or straight into the air fryer drawer if you are cooking in a dual air fryer. Add the onion and garlic and ginger paste along with a pinch of salt and pepper. Cook for 12 minutes, stirring twice during the cooking process to break up the minced meat.

**3.** Meanwhile, cook the egg noodles according to the packet instructions.

**4.** Stir the green pepper, black bean paste, soy sauce, beef stock and honey through the pork mixture, then cook for a further 5 minutes. Serve with the egg noodles and a sprinkling of spring onions.

10 MINS

 27 MINS

*Chilli con carne is honestly one of my all-time go-to comfort foods, and did you know you could create this classic in an air fryer? It's actually very simple, too. If you like, you can drain off the fat after step 2, but I think it adds to the flavour, so I'll leave it up to you. Try scattering any leftovers on tortilla chips and bake with some grated cheese for a tasty nachos lunch.*

# CHILLI CON CARNE

**SERVES 4**

400 g (14 oz) minced beef
1 onion, finely chopped
2 garlic cloves, crushed
    or finely grated
1 green pepper, deseeded
    and finely chopped
1 teaspoon smoked paprika
1 heaped teaspoon
    ground cumin
1 tablespoon dried oregano
1 teaspoon chilli powder
400 g (14 oz) can of
    chopped tomatoes
400 g (14 oz) can of kidney
    beans, drained
150 ml (¼ pint) boiling
    beef stock
1 teaspoon light brown sugar,
    or any sugar, to taste
salt and pepper

*To serve (optional)*
soured cream
sliced green chillies
tortilla chips
guacamole
grated Cheddar cheese
lime wedges

**1.** Preheat the air fryer to 200°C/400°F.

**2.** Put the minced meat into a heatproof container measuring about 20 × 15 cm (8 × 6 inches). Add the onion, garlic, pepper and spices along with a pinch of salt and pepper, stir well, then cook for 12 minutes. Drain off the fat at this point, if you like (see recipe introduction).

**3.** Pour in the tomatoes, beans and stock, then stir well. Cook for a further 15 minutes, then add sugar to taste.

**4.** Serve with soured cream, sliced green chillies, tortilla chips, guacamole, grated Cheddar cheese and lime wedges for squeezing over, if you like.

# TIME-SAVER MEALS & CHEAT INGREDIENTS

This is probably going to be everyone's favourite chapter, because who doesn't like making life easy in the kitchen? As a chef and home cook, I realize that sometimes I'm setting myself up for criticism when it comes to taking shortcuts with food, because the purists won't like it. And although I'm now 18 years into my food career, I'm still learning every single day, including about what and how people truly want to cook at home.

A quick story: I was recently approached in the street by a lovely lady who wanted to talk to me about a recipe I'd popped on to my social media. It made my day when she thanked me for creating a dish without any faff. It was a chuck-it-all-in slow-cooker recipe: I didn't brown the meat, I didn't cook the veg first, I just chucked it in. It was simple, but most of all it was tasty.

That got me thinking about who I truly write recipes for. I realized it wasn't to show off and make me look good. It was to make life easier for the people that follow me and my food. The recipes in this chapter do exactly that, they use 'cheat' ingredients – such as shop-bought pesto in my Red Pesto Chicken and Mozzarella Bake, hot honey in my Hot Honey Baked Camembert and ready-made microwaveable mash in my Cheat's Cottage Pie – to make your life a whole lot easier.

10 MINS

 10 MINS

 VEGETARIAN

*This is probably my favourite way to enjoy cheese. This oozing Camembert studded with garlic and rosemary is a classic combination, but I've added sweetness from hot chilli-infused honey, to make a perfect counterbalance to the rich cheese. Obviously you are going to need something to dip into it, so check out my Crispy Bagel Bites (see page 97).*

# HOT HONEY BAKED CAMEMBERT

**SERVES 4**

1 Camembert cheese,
  in a wooden box
2 garlic cloves, finely sliced
4 rosemary sprigs, divided
  into spriglets
1 tablespoon olive oil
1 tablespoon hot honey
½ teaspoon chilli flakes
Crispy Bagel Bites (see page
  97), to serve

**1.** Preheat the air fryer to 160°C/325°F.

**2.** Remove the Camembert from the box and remove any outer wrapping, then pop the cheese back into the box. Using a sharp knife, score the cheese in a diamond pattern, making sure to cut through the rind. Gently stick garlic slivers into some of the cuts and spriglets of rosemary into others. Drizzle with the olive oil, hot honey and chilli flakes.

**3.** Place in the air fryer drawer and cook for 10 minutes.

**4.** Serve immediately with my Crispy Bagel Bites.

5 MINS

 10 MINS

 VEGETARIAN

*The recipe you need when you're on your knees with exhaustion but craving something totally delicious. I first came across gyoza while I was cooking on MasterChef Goes Large – where I learned to make them from scratch – and I've loved them ever since. However, I've recently found amazing frozen gyoza in my local Asian supermarket, and most major supermarkets do them too, so I stock up for just these occasions. Simply serve with my ginger dipping sauce. Job done.*

# CRISPY GYOZA WITH GINGER DIPPING SAUCE

**SERVES 2**

1 bag (about 12) frozen gyoza
1 tablespoon vegetable oil
spring onion curls, to garnish

*For the dipping sauce*
2 tablespoons sweet
  chilli sauce
1 tablespoon soy sauce
1 tablespoon rice vinegar
½ teaspoon garlic and
  ginger paste

**1.** Preheat the air fryer to 180°C/350°F.

—

**2.** Place the frozen gyoza in a bowl, add the oil and stir to make sure they all have a coating of the oil. Pop on to the crisp plate inside the air fryer drawer in a single layer and cook for 10 minutes.

—

**3.** While the gyoza are cooking, put all the dipping sauce ingredients in a small bowl and stir together.

—

**4.** Garnish the crisp gyoza with the spring onion curls and serve with the dipping sauce.

—

10 MINS

15 MINS

*Egg-fried rice from the takeaway is one of my favourites, but I do often worry about the amount of oil it takes to get it just right. By making it in the air fryer, you can create this fakeaway without the guilt. I've used a time-saving pouch of microwave rice to speed up the process, but if you have some leftover rice from a previous meal, feel free to use that. Please note that if you are using cooked rice leftover from another meal, it must have been stored in the refrigerator and used within 24 hours.*

# PRAWN AIR-FRIED RICE

**SERVES 1**

250 g (9 oz) pouch of
  microwave rice
1 heaped teaspoon garlic
  and ginger paste
80 g (2¾ oz) prawns
50 g (1¾ oz) frozen peas,
  defrosted
1 small red chilli, finely sliced
3 spring onions, finely
  chopped
1 egg, lightly beaten
1 tablespoon soy sauce,
  or to taste

**1.** Preheat the air fryer to 210°C/410°F.

**2.** Tip the rice into the air fryer drawer, or a heatproof container measuring about 20 × 15 cm (8 × 6 inches). Stir through the garlic and ginger paste, prawns, peas, chilli and spring onions, then cook for 10 minutes.

**3.** Drizzle over the egg, then cook for a further 5 minutes, stirring occasionally to break up the egg. Finally add the soy sauce to taste, stir well, then serve.

### Tip

Cooked rice can harbour bacteria, so it's best to refrigerate any leftover cooked rice as soon as it is cold and eat it up quickly.

10 MINS

20 MINS

*While working at ITV on the Lorraine show, I used to share a coffee in the mornings with a lovely Irish guy called Russell Alford. He is a huge foodie who has written his own cookbook and has his own podcast as one half of the GastroGays. Russell used to go on about eating a 'spice bag' at takeaways in Ireland. I had no idea what this was until I travelled there and tried one. As soon as I dug in to this bag filled with spicy chips and chicken with fried onions and peppers, I realized what the fuss was about. It was so good. Please forgive me, my Irish friends, I know my version is not authentic, but it's lush.*

# POPCORN CHICKEN SPICE BAG

**SERVES 2**

300 g (10½ oz) shop-bought frozen chips
½ red pepper, deseeded and chopped
½ green pepper, deseeded and chopped
½ onion, chopped
200 g (7 oz) frozen popcorn chicken
1 tablespoon vegetable oil
1 teaspoon garlic powder
¼ teaspoon Chinese 5 spice
½ teaspoon chilli powder
½ teaspoon sweet paprika
1 teaspoon salt
curry sauce, to serve (optional)

**1.** Preheat the air fryer to 190°C/375°F.

**2.** Scatter the chips, peppers, onion and popcorn chicken into the air fryer drawer, then drizzle over the oil, scatter in the spices and salt and shake well or stir to combine.

**3.** Cook for 20 minutes, shaking a couple of times during cooking, then serve immediately, with curry sauce for drizzling on top, if you like.

10 MINS

 22 MINS

*Red pesto gets its distinctive colour and flavour from both sun-dried tomatoes and red peppers. Luckily, you can buy great-tasting red pesto in most supermarkets these days and I've used it here to pimp up a delicious chicken recipe. Depending on what I fancy, sometimes I enjoy this with pasta, or at other times some beautifully crisp rosemary-spiked potatoes.*

# RED PESTO CHICKEN & MOZZARELLA BAKE

**SERVES 4**

4 skinless, boneless
   chicken thighs, cut
   into bite-sized pieces
1 small red onion,
   finely chopped
1 teaspoon garlic paste
splash of oil
400 g (14 oz) can of
   chopped tomatoes
1 heaped tablespoon
   red pesto
1 tablespoon balsamic
   vinegar
100 g (3½ oz) ready-grated
   mozzarella cheese
salt and pepper

**1.** Preheat the air fryer to 200°C/400°F.

**2.** Place the chicken, onion and garlic paste in a bowl, then add the splash of oil, season with salt and pepper and mix well to coat. Tip the chicken into a heatproof dish measuring about 20 × 15 cm (8 × 6 inches), pop it into your air fryer drawer and cook for 10 minutes, stirring halfway through.

**3.** After 10 minutes, stir, then add in the tomatoes, pesto and balsamic and mix well. Return to the air fryer and cook for a further 12 minutes. Halfway through the cooking time, stir, then scatter over the mozzarella and return to the air fryer to finish cooking.

20 MINS

 37 MINS

*There's something heavenly about crisp pastry layers with a rich filling sandwiched in between. Let's be honest: unless you're in training for The Great British Bake Off, you're not going be making puff pastry at home. In my opinion, this needs nothing more than a lovely dollop of brown sauce on the side. Happy days.*

# CHICKEN & MUSHROOM SLICE

**SERVES 4**

2 skinless, boneless chicken thighs, finely chopped (total weight about 150 g/ 5½ oz)

150 g (5½ oz) mushrooms, sliced

1 teaspoon garlic granules

1 teaspoon dried thyme

1 tablespoon oil

80 g (2¾ oz) cream cheese

1 sheet shop-bought ready-rolled puff pastry, measuring about 36 × 24 cm (14¼ × 9½ inches)

1 egg, lightly beaten

salt and pepper

**1.** Preheat the air fryer to 200°C/400°F.

**2.** Put the chicken, mushrooms, garlic granules, thyme and oil in the air fryer drawer and mix to combine. Cook for 12 minutes, stirring halfway through, then leave to cool.

**3.** Once cooled, mix through the cream cheese and season with salt and pepper.

**4.** Cut the pastry into 8 rectangles, each measuring about 12 × 9 cm (4½ × 3½ inches). Lay 4 rectangles on a work surface, then divide the chicken filling between them, making sure to leave a 1 cm (½ inch) border all around. Brush this border with a little of the beaten egg, then top each with another pastry rectangle. Use a fork to crimp the edges together to seal, then trim them to neaten up, if you like. Make a couple of holes in the top of the slices, then brush with the rest of the egg.

**5.** Reduce the air fryer temperature to 160°C/325°F. Place the slices on the crisp plate in the air fryer drawer, then bake for 25 minutes until crisp and golden.

**5 MINS**

 **14 MINS**

*Have you ever brunched on a croque monsieur? If so, you'll know it's a wonderful French toasted sandwich of ham and cheese with cheesy creamy béchamel, better known as white sauce in the UK. You can buy jars of white sauce in any local supermarket. I love a good cheat in the kitchen, so I've used the shop-bought sauce to create a Spanish, air fryer take on this classic dish.*

# CROQUE SEÑOR TOASTIE

**MAKES 1**

2 crusty white bread slices
1 tablespoon chilli jam
5 thin chorizo slices
100 g (3½ oz) shop-bought
 béchamel sauce
60 g (2¼ oz) Cheddar
 cheese, grated

**1.** Preheat the air fryer to 190°C/375°F.

**2.** Butter the bread, then place on the crisp plate inside the air fryer drawer and cook for 4 minutes.

**3.** Remove from the air fryer and spread the chilli jam over one slice of the bread, then lay on the chorizo. Add a layer of about half the béchamel sauce, then sprinkle on half the cheese. Pop the second slice of bread on top, then add another layer of béchamel and cheese, making sure you go right to the edges.

**4.** Return the sandwich to the crisp plate in the air fryer drawer and cook for 10 minutes until golden and bubbling.

**Tip**

As with any toastie you make in the air fryer, if you are finding that the top slice of bread lifts up while cooking, then pop a couple of cocktail sticks through the sandwich to secure it in place, or rest a wire rack on top.

10 MINS

 22 MINS

*When you want to eat something completely decadent without making much effort, this cheesy bake is a game-changer. If you have never tried gnocchi, this is a great opportunity to give it a go. I've often seen it boiled, but when baked it's so much better. It also has a long shelf life, so it makes for a perfect standby when you want to get dinner on the table with next-to-no effort.*

# CRISPY GNOCCHI CHEESE BAKE

**SERVES 2**

1 × 500 g (1 lb 2 oz) pack
 of potato gnocchi
90 g (3¼ oz) bacon lardons
½ tablespoon olive oil
410 g (14½ oz) can of
 evaporated milk
100 g (3½ oz) Cheddar
 cheese, grated, plus
 more for topping
100 g (3½ oz) ready-grated
 mozzarella cheese, plus
 more for topping
handful of chives,
 finely chopped
salt and pepper
green salad, to serve

**1.** Preheat the air fryer to 200°C/400°F.

**2.** Scatter the gnocchi and bacon lardons into a heatproof container measuring about 20 × 15 cm (8 × 6 inches), drizzle over the oil and toss well. Season with salt and pepper. Place in the air fryer drawer, then cook for 10 minutes, tossing every few minutes.

**3.** In a bowl, mix together the evaporated milk and cheeses. Pour this over the gnocchi, then return to the air fryer and cook for a further 12 minutes. Halfway through, give it a stir, then scatter over a little more cheese for topping.

**4.** Leave to cool for a couple of minutes, then sprinkle over the chives and serve with a green salad.

**5 MINS**

 **12 MINS**

*Luckily enough we can find harissa, the smoky spiced North African chilli paste, in most supermarkets these days. My favourite contains fragrant rose petals and it's a revelation. Harissa is so versatile – you can use it in dressings, marinades and sauces – but it's an especially incredible combination with lamb. Just serve these chops with a drizzle of yogurt and some pomegranate seeds for the win! They also work perfectly with my Batata Harra (Spicy Lebanese Roast Potatoes, see page 148).*

# HARISSA-SPICED LAMB CHOPS

**SERVES 2**

4 lamb loin chops
1 tablespoon rose
   harissa paste
½ teaspoon salt
1 teaspoon ground cumin
1 teaspoon honey

*To serve*
natural yogurt, drizzled with
   extra harissa paste
pomegranate seeds
Batata Harra (see page 148)

**1.** Preheat the air fryer to 210°C/410°F.

**2.** Pop the lamb chops in a bowl, then add the harissa paste, salt, cumin and honey. Rub well to make sure the lamb is well coated.

**3.** Place on the crisp plate inside the air fryer drawer. Cook for 12 minutes, turning halfway through.

**4.** Serve with yogurt, pomegranate seeds and my Batata Harra.

10 MINS

34 MINS

*The purists are going to tell me to hide away and never show my face again after seeing what I've done to this classic British dish. But I make no apologies for making this recipe so simple that it almost feels like cheating. It's about time we stopped feeling guilty for making our lives easier when we are up against it. With a dish like this, for instance, why not save time by using gravy granules and ready-made mashed potatoes? Enjoy with some buttered greens on the side.*

# CHEAT'S COTTAGE PIE

## SERVES 4

500 g (1 lb 2 oz) minced beef
1 carrot, very finely chopped
1 onion, finely chopped
400 ml (14 fl oz) beef gravy, made from granules
1 teaspoon dried thyme
1 heaped teaspoon wholegrain mustard
1 large (about 800 g/ 1 lb 12 oz) pack of shop-bought mashed potato
100 g (3½ oz) Cheddar cheese, grated
salt and pepper
buttered greens, to serve

**1.** Preheat the air fryer to 200°C/400°F.

**2.** Put the minced beef, carrot, onion and a pinch of salt and pepper into a heatproof baking dish measuring about 20 × 15 cm (8 × 6 inches). Cook in the air fryer drawer for 12 minutes, stirring twice during the cooking process to break up the mince.

**3.** Pour in the gravy, then stir through the thyme and mustard and mix well. Return the dish to the air fryer for 12 minutes.

**4.** Meanwhile, microwave the mashed potato according to the packet instructions.

**5.** Spread the warmed mashed potato over the mince, using a fork to create some texture, then sprinkle over the cheese and cook for a further 10 minutes until the potato topping is crisp.

**6.** Serve immediately with the buttered greens.

# ON THE SIDE

A side dish can make or break a meal. We're living in times of ultimate convenience, where you can buy a lot of ready-made side dishes in the supermarkets. However, these are never cheap and they never *ever* taste as good as the homemade versions.

I just love it when I see food going viral on the internet and my Cajun-Spiced New Potatoes are a nod to a recipe which I think every single air fryer fan must have now made at some point or another. I believe that this was successful because it took a simple and often underused ingredient – canned new potatoes – then spiced them up and cooked them until beautifully crisp in an air fryer. Simple and ingenious.

On the other hand, there are side dishes that require just a little more effort, but the results are spectacular. So why not give my Batata Harra (Spicy Lebanese Roast Potatoes) and my famous Creamy Leek and Cabbage Gratin – which everyone requests when they come to dinner at our house – a try?

There's also an outlier here: Crispy Harissa Chickpeas. They had to go in, first because harissa is one of my favourite ingredients, and second because they're one of the few things that stop my wife Liz always complaining that she's hungry between meals...

 30 MINS

 20-25 MINS

 VEGETARIAN

*Roast potatoes are a staple and, actually, my favourite part of a British Sunday roast... so much so that they can make or break the meal for me. Cooking them in the air fryer has taken my roasters to a whole new level, with the added bonus of using only a fraction of the usual amount of oil. These spicy Lebanese potatoes are an absolute revelation: think of them as roast potato 2.0. They are going to blow your mind. I like to serve them with my Harissa-Spiced Lamb Chops (see page 142) for a spicy spin on the Sunday roast.*

# BATATA HARRA SPICY LEBANESE ROAST POTATOES

**SERVES 4**

800 g (1 lb 12 oz) Maris Piper potatoes, peeled and quartered
1 teaspoon salt, plus more to parboil the potatoes
1 teaspoon ground turmeric
1 teaspoon ground cumin
1 teaspoon chilli flakes
1 teaspoon mustard seeds
1 tablespoon oil

*To serve*
small bunch of dill, torn
1 green chilli, finely sliced

**1.** Preheat the air fryer to 200°C/400°F.

**2.** Parboil the potatoes in boiling salted water for 8 minutes, then drain and leave to steam in a colander for 5 minutes. Transfer to a large mixing bowl.

**3.** Mix the 1 teaspoon of salt and the spices together in a small bowl, then sprinkle this over the potatoes. Drizzle over the oil, then gently shake the bowl to rough up the potatoes.

**4.** Place the potatoes in the air fryer drawer, then cook for 20–25 minutes, shaking from time to time, until crisp.

**5.** Sprinkle over the dill and green chilli, then serve.

10 MINS

 24 MINS

 VEGETARIAN

*One of my all-time favourite recipes, inspired by a special restaurant in my home town of Bristol called Pasture, an incredible steakhouse. It was even on the menu at my wedding to my beautiful wife Liz. It's so easy to make and the bonus is you can make it seasonal, by using whatever greens you like. During the winter, why not try cavolo nero, or when the weather warms up, spring greens go down a treat. In the summer, serve with sugar snap peas.*

# CREAMY LEEK & CABBAGE GRATIN

**SERVES 4**

240 g (8½ oz) leek, shredded
100 g (3½ oz) cabbage, shredded
2 garlic cloves, crushed or finely grated
1 tablespoon oil
1 teaspoon wholegrain mustard
300 ml (½ pint) double cream
150 g (5½ oz) Cheddar cheese, grated
40 g (1½ oz) breadcrumbs
salt and pepper
seasonal greens, to serve

**1.** Preheat the air fryer to 170°C/340°F.

**2.** Tip the leek, cabbage and garlic into the air fryer drawer, then drizzle over the oil, add a pinch of salt and pepper and mix well. Cook for 12 minutes.

**3.** Put the cooked vegetables into a mixing bowl, then add the mustard, cream and most of the cheese, reserving some for the top. Mix well, then transfer to a baking dish measuring about 18 × 12 cm (7 × 4½ inches), or two smaller dishes.

**4.** Increase the air fryer temperature to 200°C/400°F. Sprinkle over the remaining cheese and breadcrumbs, then place the dish in the air fryer drawer and cook for a further 12 minutes.

**5.** Serve warm with your choice of seasonal greens.

5 MINS

 15 MINS

 VEGETARIAN

*If you have been following me and my recipes for a while, you will know I'm a huge fan of a canned potato. I literally lived on them when I was a student. I used to put them in everything; they went into curries and stews, or were just simply coated in a bit of butter and black pepper. They were so good and so cheap. And then I saw a viral air fryer canned potato recipe on TikTok and I just had to try it. I love this Cajun-spiced version, but feel free to experiment with your own spice blend.*

# CAJUN-SPICED NEW POTATOES

**SERVES 4**

2 × 500 g (1 lb 2 oz) cans of new potatoes, drained
2 tablespoons oil
1 tablespoon garlic granules
1 heaped teaspoon dried oregano
½ teaspoon chilli powder
1 heaped teaspoon smoked paprika
1 tablespoon plain flour
salt and pepper

**1.** Preheat the air fryer to 200°C/400°F.

**2.** Pop the potatoes into the air fryer drawer, then drizzle over the oil and toss to coat. Sprinkle in the garlic, oregano, spices and flour, then add a good pinch of salt and pepper. Toss again to make sure the potatoes are coated, then cook for 15 minutes, tossing a couple of times more while they cook.

35 MINS

 48 MINS

 VEGETARIAN

*Garlic bread has to be one of the greatest culinary inventions ever. There's not a meal out there that can't be improved by having a bit of this crunchy, golden loaf on the side. Whether it's to mop up your Spaghetti Bolognese sauce (see page 112) or dip into my melting Hot Honey Baked Camembert (see page 128), you will be onto a winner with this classic side dish.*

# PULL APART ROASTED GARLIC & CHILLI BREAD

## SERVES 4

2 large bulbs of garlic
2 tablespoons olive oil
250 g (9 oz) salted butter, softened
2 teaspoons chilli flakes
4 tablespoons finely chopped parsley
1 loaf that fits in your air fryer drawer, a small sourdough or ciabatta would be ideal

**1.** Preheat the air fryer to 190°C/375°F.

**2.** Cut the top off each bulb of garlic to expose the cloves inside. Place each bulb (cut side up) on a piece of foil, drizzle with oil, then bring the sides of the foil up and over to totally enclose the garlic. Place the wrapped garlic bulbs on the crisp plate inside your air fryer drawer. Cook for 40 minutes then leave to cool for 15 minutes. When cool, unwrap each bulb and squeeze the softened garlic into a bowl. Mix in the butter, chilli flakes and parsley.

**3.** Make cuts in the loaf approximately 2.5 cm (1 inch) apart in a diamond pattern, being careful not to cut all of the way through. Spread the garlic butter generously within the cuts, then pop the loaf into your air fryer drawer. Cook at 180°C/375°F for 8 minutes.

### Tip
If you have any garlic butter left over, cover and store in the fridge for another time.

5 MINS

 15 MINS

 VEGETARIAN

*These crispy chickpeas make such a delicious snack. My wife Liz constantly moans that she is hungry... luckily, she has me on hand to help with that and these nibbles are great for taking the edge off your peckishness. I also toss these on top of soup instead of croutons, for added texture. They are delicious on my Roasted Red Pepper and Harissa Soup (see page 32).*

# CRISPY HARISSA CHICKPEAS

**SERVES 4**

---

400 g (14 oz) can of
　chickpeas drained
1 tablespoon olive oil
½ teaspoon ground cumin
½ teaspoon salt
½ teaspoon dried oregano
1 teaspoon rose harissa

**1.** Preheat the air fryer to 200°C/400°F.

---

**2.** Tip the chickpeas into a bowl, drizzle with the oil, then stir through the cumin, salt, oregano and harissa. Scatter onto the crisp plate in your air fryer drawer, then cook for 15 minutes until crisp, shaking several times during cooking.

---

15 MINS

 25 MINS

 VEGETARIAN

*This recipe is ideal if you have a dual drawer air fryer. I've often spoken about my passion for Spanish food, and it doesn't get more classic than this delicious potato dish. Crispy, fluffy bites of potato topped with a sweet and spicy tomato sauce, and always – for me – served with aioli (garlic mayonnaise). If you're in the mood for a bit of tapas, this dish works brilliantly with my Gambas Pil Pil with Smoky Chorizo (see page 98).*

# PATATAS BRAVAS

**SERVES 4**

600 g (1 lb 5 oz) Maris Piper
    potatoes, cut into 2.5 cm
    (1 inch) cubes
2 tablespoons oil
1 teaspoon smoked paprika
1 teaspoon garlic granules
salt and pepper

*For the bravas sauce*
1 red onion, finely chopped
2 garlic cloves, crushed
    or finely grated
1 tablespoon oil
400 g (14 oz) can of
    chopped tomatoes
½ teaspoon smoked paprika
½ red chilli, finely chopped
1 teaspoon sugar, or to taste
salt and pepper

*To serve*
2 tablespoons chopped
    flat leaf parsley leaves
chilli flakes
garlic mayonnaise

**1.** Preheat the air fryer to 180°C/350°F.

**2.** For the bravas sauce, put the onion, garlic and oil in the air fryer drawer and cook for 5 minutes. Add the tomatoes and spices, mix well, then cook for a further 15 minutes. Season with salt and pepper, then with the sugar, to taste.

**3.** If you have a dual air fryer, scatter the cubed potatoes into the second air fryer drawer, dress with the oil, then add the paprika, garlic granules and a good pinch of salt and pepper. Cook for 20 minutes, shaking every 5 minutes. If you don't have a dual air fryer, you can cook the sauce first, then reheat it to serve, or even make it in a saucepan on the stove in the same way.

**4.** Once cooked, spoon the sauce over the crispy potatoes, then sprinkle over the parsley and chilli flakes and serve with garlic mayo.

**Tip**

This also works great using the canned new potatoes and method from my Cajun-Spiced New Potatoes (see page 152).

15 MINS

 40 MINS

 VEGETARIAN

*One of the first classic recipes I learned to cook back in the day was this beautiful French potato dish. I don't think it can be beaten when it comes to total indulgence. It looks equally at home as part of a Sunday roast as it does if you are trying your hand at a bit of fine dining to impress your mates. I make two smaller servings to fit inside my dual air fryer drawers, but you can also make one big dish instead, to save on the washing up.*

# DAUPHINOISE POTATOES

## SERVES 4

600 g (1 lb 5 oz) Maris
   Piper potatoes, peeled
2 garlic cloves, crushed
   or finely grated
1 teaspoon dried thyme
200 ml (7 fl oz) double cream
100 ml (3 ½fl oz) whole milk
salt and pepper

**1.** Preheat the air fryer to 160°C/325°F.

**2.** Finely slice the potatoes: a mandolin does this with ease, but watch those fingers! Choose some suitable baking dishes; either a large dish measuring about 25 × 18 cm (10 × 7 inches), or two smaller dishes measuring 18 × 12 cm (7 × 4½ inches). Layer the potatoes, seasoning every few layers with salt and pepper and a small scattering of the garlic and thyme, then pour over the cream and milk, making sure the potatoes are just covered.

**3.** Place the baking dish(es) into the air fryer drawer and cook for 40 minutes.

### Tip

It's essential to have baking dishes that will fit into your air fryer. I usually use the same dishes in my dual air fryer, but make sure you know the internal dimensions of your model before you splash out on any new dishes.

10 MINS

 22 MINS

 VEGETARIAN

*These Indian-spiced potatoes are absolutely incredible and it's a huge bonus that you can do them from start to finish in the air fryer. Gram flour – made from chickpeas and easily found in supermarkets' world food aisles – will help the potatoes become beautifully crisp. I also like to leave the skin on, for extra crunch, and serve up with a mint and coriander yogurt drizzle. Absolutely banging! These are great on the side with my Chicken Tikka (see page 100).*

# GUNPOWDER POTATOES

**SERVES 2**

500 g (1 lb 2 oz) Maris Piper potatoes, cut into 2 cm (¾ inch) cubes
1 tablespoon oil
1 tablespoon gram flour
½ teaspoon ground turmeric
1 teaspoon garam masala
1 teaspoon ground cumin
½ teaspoon chilli flakes
1 teaspoon mustard seeds
salt and pepper

**1.** Preheat the air fryer to 170°C/340°F.

**2.** Stick all the ingredients in a bowl and add a good pinch of salt and pepper. Mix well until the potatoes have a coating of seasoning, then scatter them into the air fryer drawer and cook for 12 minutes, shaking halfway through.

**3.** Increase the air fryer temperature to 200°C/400°F, then cook for a further 10 minutes, again shaking halfway through.

5 MINS

 20 MINS

 VEGETARIAN

*Roasted broccoli is great! Remember those days when we used to boil it until it almost fell apart? I'm so glad we have evolved to treat vegetables with the respect that they deserve. Broccoli has a wonderful texture and flavour when it's cooked in the air fryer and – let's be honest – everything tastes better with a seasoning of cheese. This makes a great side dish with my Roast Crackling Pork (see page 63).*

# GARLIC & PARMESAN BROCCOLI

**SERVES 4**

1 head of broccoli,
   cut into florets
1 tablespoon oil
1 teaspoon garlic granules
½ teaspoon chilli flakes
50 g (1¾ oz) Parmesan
   cheese, finely grated
salt and pepper

**1.** Preheat the air fryer to 180°C/350°F.

**2.** Pop the broccoli florets into a bowl, then drizzle in the oil and toss to coat. Sprinkle in the garlic and chilli flakes, then season with salt and pepper. Tip into the air fryer drawer, then cook for 10 minutes.

**3.** Shake well, then scatter in the Parmesan cheese and return to the air fryer to cook for a further 10 minutes.

10 MINS

 18 MINS

 VEGETARIAN

*It's time to pimp up your fries game! These are the ultimate snack on their own, or side to Wes's Favourite Sweet-and-Sour Chicken (see page 62). Of course, you can make your own fries, but – let's be honest – we all have a bag of frozen chips in the freezer. My one bit of advice would be to go easy on the 5 spice, as too much can be overpowering.*

# SALT & PEPPER FRIES

**SERVES 2**

300 g (10½ oz) frozen chips
½ teaspoon sea salt flakes
½ teaspoon cracked
 black pepper
¼ teaspoon Chinese 5 spice
½ teaspoon chilli flakes
½ red pepper, deseeded
 and finely chopped
1 green pepper, deseeded
 and finely chopped
½ red chilli, finely sliced
1 tablespoon oil
sweet chilli sauce, to serve

**1.** Preheat the air fryer to 200°C/400°F.

—

**2.** Scatter all the ingredients into the air fryer drawer, then shake well or stir to combine. Cook for 18 minutes, shaking regularly. Serve with sweet chilli sauce for dipping.

—

10 MINS

 28 MINS

*The cheeses in this recipe are just my suggestions: in fact, for this recipe, you can use whatever cheese you have lying around in the refrigerator. Have you ever wondered what to do with all that cheese left over from the festive period? Well, this bake is perfect for using it up. Depending on the size of your air fryer, you can either make one large bake or two smaller ones.*

# CAULIFLOWER, BACON & BLUE CHEESE BAKE

**SERVES 4**

1 cauliflower, cut into florets
1 tablespoon oil
90 g (3¼ oz) smoked
  bacon lardons
300 ml (½ pint) double
  cream
1 tablespoon Dijon mustard
100 g (3½ oz) Cheddar
  cheese, grated
50 g (1¾ oz) blue cheese,
  crumbled or grated
salt and pepper
steamed broccoli, to serve

**1.** Preheat the air fryer to 170°C/340°F.

**2.** Pop the cauliflower florets into the air fryer drawer and drizzle over the oil, season with salt and pepper – not too much salt, because of the cheese and bacon – and mix well. Cook for 8 minutes.

**3.** Add the bacon lardons, then cook for another 8 minutes.

**4.** Tip the cauliflower and bacon into a bowl, then add the cream, mustard and most of the cheese, reserving some for the top. Mix well, then transfer to 1 large or 2 small heatproof dishes, depending on the size of your air fryer. (A large dish would measure about 25 × 18 cm/10 × 7 inches and small dishes about 18 × 12 cm/7 × 4½ inches.) Sprinkle over the remaining cheese, then cook for a further 12 minutes.

**5.** Serve warm with steamed broccoli on the side.

# SOMETHING SWEET

I've got such a sweet tooth that not a single day goes by without some sort of treat passing my lips. So, this was the chapter that was the most fun for me, while I was developing the recipes. Luckily for me, and my dentist, I had a little helper too: my daughter. Indie loves to cook desserts and these delicious recipes, such as my Banana & Chocolate Chip Muffins and Gooey S'mores Turnovers, were a pleasure to make (and eat) together.

The air fryer once more shows its versatility when you're cooking sweet recipes. Not only can you recreate your favourite baked or fried desserts, but you can also use the gentler settings and cooking functions to knock-up recipes that would traditionally need a lower conventional oven temperature, such as a delicious batch of Daim Bar Chocolate Cookies, or rich Caramel Egg Brownie Pots.

An absolute standout recipe for me in this chapter is my Chocolate Salted Caramel Pudding, which to me showcases everything great about the air fryer. Not only does it turn out a beautifully moist sponge, but also the chocolate salted caramel sauce that is drizzled over the top. Trust me: you are going to need to try that one.

15 MINS

 15 MINS

 VEGETARIAN

*This dish was born from my love for French toast and it has the classic flavour combinations you associate with that breakfast dish, though I love it as a dessert. It's also a great way to use up any stale croissants you may have lurking in the bread bin.*

# FRENCH TOAST CROISSANT BAKE

**SERVES 4**

3 eggs, lightly beaten
50 g (1¾ oz) caster sugar
¼ teaspoon ground cinnamon
100 ml (3½ fl oz) milk
butter, for the dish
3 large croissants, torn into pieces (total weight about 200 g/7 oz)
70 g (2½ oz) blueberries
double cream, to serve

**1.** Preheat the air fryer to 160°C/325°F.

**2.** In a bowl, whisk together the eggs, sugar, cinnamon and milk until fully combined. Butter a heatproof baking dish measuring about 20 × 15 cm (8 × 6 inches). Place the croissant pieces in the prepared dish, then pour over the egg mixture. Leave to sit for 5 minutes, then scatter over the blueberries, tucking a few of the berries in among the croissants.

**3.** Place the dish into the air fryer drawer and cook for 15 minutes. Serve with a drizzle of double cream.

5 MINS

 8 MINS

 VEGETARIAN

*This is the ultimate lazy dessert, which can be on the table and in your belly in less than 10 minutes. When I was a kid, we all loved a banana split, fully loaded up with cream, ice cream, chocolate and sprinkles and – of course – a fluorescent glacé cherry plonked on the top. This is my air fryer nod to that classic, but much simpler. Paired with its easy 30-second microwave chocolate sauce, this dessert is a beauty.*

# BRÛLÉED BANANA SPLIT WITH HOT CHOCOLATE SAUCE

**SERVES 2**

2 ripe bananas
1 tablespoon caster sugar

**For the chocolate sauce**
30 g (1 oz) dark
    chocolate chips
1 tablespoon boiling water
1 heaped teaspoon instant
    coffee granules (optional)

**To serve**
ice cream
colourful sprinkles

**1.** Preheat the air fryer to 200°C/400°F.

**2.** While the bananas are still in their skins, cut them in half lengthways. Sprinkle the cut sides evenly with the sugar, place on the crisp plate inside the air fryer drawer and cook for 8 minutes.

**3.** Meanwhile, make the chocolate sauce. Weigh the ingredients into a small microwaveable bowl, place in the microwave and heat on full power for 30 seconds. Stir well until smooth.

**4.** Serve the bananas – still in their skins – with a dollop of ice cream, a drizzle of the hot chocolate sauce and some colourful sprinkles.

55 MINS

 52 MINS

 VEGETARIAN

*Baking in the air fryer is an absolute revelation and I've used it to my full advantage to create a dessert which showcases one of my favourite flavour combinations. For me, the only thing that improves salted caramel is a hit of chocolate. You will definitely need to serve this with either a drizzle of double cream or a nice dollop of clotted cream.*

# CHOCOLATE SALTED CARAMEL PUDDING

### SERVES 2

60 g (2¼ oz) pitted
 dates, chopped
50 ml (1¾ fl oz) boiling water
30 g (1 oz) unsalted butter,
 plus more for the dish
50 g (1¾ oz) dark
 muscovado sugar
1 egg
40 g (1½ oz) black treacle
60 g (2¼ oz) self-raising flour
1 tablespoon cocoa powder
⅓ teaspoon bicarbonate
 of soda
50 g (1¾ oz) dark
 chocolate chips

#### For the sauce
40 g (1½ oz) unsalted butter
40 g (1½ oz) dark
 chocolate chips
40 g (1½ oz) dark
 muscovado sugar
50 ml (1¾ fl oz) double
 cream, plus more to serve
½ teaspoon sea salt flakes,
 or to taste

**1.** Soak the dates in a bowl with the boiling water for 30 minutes, then use the back of a fork to break them down.

**2.** Meanwhile, make the sauce. Preheat the air fryer to 200°C/400°F. Pop the butter, chocolate chips, sugar and cream into the air fryer drawer and cook for 8 minutes, stirring a couple of times along the way. Add the salt to taste. Transfer the sauce to a bowl.

**3.** Reduce the air fryer temperature to 150°C/300°F and butter a heatproof dish measuring about 18 × 14 cm (7 × 5½ inches).

**4.** In a bowl with an electric whisk, or in a food mixer fitted with the whisk attachment, cream together the butter and sugar, then beat in the egg. Whisk through the treacle, then sift in the flour, cocoa and bicarbonate of soda and whisk again. Lastly, fold through the dates and chocolate chips.

**5.** Spoon the pudding mix into the prepared dish, then place in your air fryer drawer and cook for 25 minutes.

**6.** Serve the sponge with a good helping of the reheated chocolate salted caramel sauce and a drizzle of cream.

10 MINS

 20 MINS

 VEGETARIAN

*S'mores have been popping up all over my social media for a long, long time, and there's a good reason for that: the combination of rich chocolate, gooey marshmallow and crisp biscuit make this the perfect bite when you are craving something sweet. I've replaced the biscuit element with some crisp shop-bought puff pastry here. Once baked until golden in the air fryer, you have a quick and easy dessert that the family will demolish in mere minutes.*

# GOOEY S'MORES TURNOVERS

**MAKES 4**

1 sheet of shop-bought ready-rolled puff pastry, measuring about 22 × 22 cm (8½ × 8½ inches)
100 g (3½ oz) chocolate and hazelnut spread
about 30 mini marshmallows
1 egg, lightly beaten
icing sugar, to dust

**1.** Preheat the air fryer to 160°C/325°F.

**2.** Cut the pastry into four 11cm (4¼ inch) squares. Spread on the chocolate spread, leaving a 1 cm (½ inch) border all the way round, then place a spoonful of mini marshmallows on each pastry square. Brush the border with beaten egg, then lift one corner of each square and press it down on to the opposite corner to form a triangle-shaped pastry. Use a fork to crimp the edges together, then trim to neaten, if you like. Make a couple of holes in the top of each turnover, then brush with the remaining egg wash.

**3.** Place the turnovers on a sheet of baking paper placed on the crisp plate in the air fryer drawer. Bake for 20 minutes until crisp and golden. Before serving, dust with icing sugar.

10 MINS

 12 MINS

 VEGETARIAN

*What do you do with bananas that are on the turn? These mini doughnuts are just so good and have so few ingredients that they are a super-easy way to throw together a lovely treat. I drizzle mine with melted Biscoff spread, which works beautifully with bananas.*

# MINI BANANA DOUGHNUT BITES

**MAKES 12**

2 over-ripe bananas, mashed
200 g (7 oz) Greek yogurt
280 g (10 oz) self-raising
    flour, plus more if needed
50 g (1¾ oz) unsalted
    butter, melted
caster sugar, to dust
melted Biscoff spread,
    to serve (optional)

**1.** Preheat the air fryer to 190°C/375°F.

**2.** In a bowl, mix together the banana, yogurt and flour until combined, then knead on a work surface for 3 minutes, adding a touch more flour if it's too sticky. Shape into 12 equal-sized balls, then pop on to a sheet of baking paper in your air fryer drawer.

**3.** Brush the balls with some of the melted butter, then cook for 12 minutes. Once cooked, brush with a little more butter, then dust with the sugar. Drizzle with Biscoff spread, if you like, then serve.

10 MINS

 45 MINS

 VEGETARIAN

*It's always handy to be able to knock up a dessert out of store cupboard ingredients and things you have in the freezer. Frozen berries and canned fruit are fantastic for these occasions. My air fryer take on a classic fruit crumble only needs to be served with some double cream or custard. Enjoy.*

# BLACK CHERRY-BERRY CRUMBLE

**SERVES 4**

410 g (14½ oz) can of black cherries in syrup
250 g (9 oz) frozen berries
double cream or custard, to serve

**For the crumble topping**
40 g (1½ oz) plain flour
40 g (1½ oz) unsalted butter, chopped
40 g (1½ oz) caster sugar
40 g (1½ oz) rolled oats

**1.** Preheat the air fryer to 200°C/400°F.

**2.** Tip the canned cherries and their syrup and the frozen berries into a heatproof baking dish measuring about 20 × 15 cm (8 × 6 inches). Cook for 20 minutes, stirring a few times along the way.

**3.** To make the crumble topping, rub together the flour and butter in a bowl with your fingertips until the mix resembles crumbs, then stir in the sugar and oats. Gently scatter it over the cherry mix, but do not compact it down or it will turn cakey, rather than staying light and crumbly.

**4.** Reduce the air fryer temperature to 180°C/350°F, then continue to cook for a further 25 minutes until golden and bubbling.

**5.** Serve warm with double cream or custard.

45 MINS

 7 MINS

 VEGETARIAN

*I love an easy bake and there's nothing better than a homemade biscuit. Shortbread has always been a particular favourite of mine, and this buttery biscuit is so light it almost melts in the mouth. Lightly flavoured, with lemon zest for added zing, alongside a cup of tea this definitely takes some beating.*

# LEMONY SHORTBREAD BISCUITS

**MAKES 24**

150 g (5½ oz) unsalted butter, chopped
55 g (2 oz) caster sugar, plus more to dust
200 g (7 oz) plain flour, plus more to dust
finely grated zest of ½ lemon

**1.** Put all the ingredients in a bowl and use your fingertips to rub in the butter until the mixture resembles crumbs, then squeeze it all together until it resembles a dough.

**2.** Roll out on a lightly floured surface until 1 cm (½ inch) thick, then use a cutter to stamp out biscuits (I use a 5 cm/ 2 inch round cutter). Re-roll the trimmings to use up all the dough. Place the biscuits on a tray lined with baking paper, then pop into the refrigerator for 30 minutes.

**3.** Preheat the air fryer to 190°C/375°F.

**4.** Remove the biscuits from the refrigerator, then use a fork to prick some holes in the surface of each. Scatter evenly with caster sugar.

**5.** Place on a sheet of baking paper in the air fryer drawer and cook 7 minutes. You may have to cook these in batches, depending on the size of your air fryer. Leave to cool on a rack before enjoying with a cup of tea.

15 MINS

 15 MINS

 VEGETARIAN

*I do love an easy baking recipe, the sort that just gets stirred together and baked until golden and delicious. These muffins are a perfect treat for the kids, or for enjoying yourself with a lovely cup of tea. So don't chuck away those really sweet over-ripe bananas; make sure to use them in this recipe.*

# BANANA & CHOCOLATE CHIP MUFFINS

**MAKES 6**

1 large over-ripe banana
100 g (3½ oz) unsalted
   butter, at room
   temperature
100 g (3½ oz) caster sugar
2 eggs
180 g (6 oz) self-raising flour
40 g (1½ oz) desiccated
   coconut
40 g (1½ oz) dark chocolate
   chips, plus more for
   topping

**1.** Preheat the air fryer to 160°C/325°F.

**2.** Peel and mash the banana in a small bowl, then set aside. In a bowl with an electric whisk, or in a food mixer fitted with the whisk attachment, cream together the butter and sugar, then beat in the eggs one at a time until fully incorporated. Fold through the mashed the banana. Sift in the flour then fold the ingredients together. Gently stir through the coconut and chocolate chips.

**3.** Divide the mixture between 6 silicone muffin cases, scatter with a few more chocolate chips, then place into the air fryer drawer and cook for 15 minutes.

25 MINS

 15 MINS

 VEGETARIAN

*This is my go-to air fryer dessert for an indulgent chocolate fix. These gooey pots of heaven are equally at home when you've got your pyjamas on, watching a good box set on TV, or at a dinner party – when you're hopefully fully dressed! – with friends and family. The addition of the caramel egg elevates this recipe.*

# CARAMEL EGG BROWNIE POTS

**SERVES 4**

160 g (5¾ oz) dark chocolate, broken into pieces
120 g (4¼ oz) unsalted butter, plus more for the ramekins
2 eggs
100 g (3½ oz) caster sugar
60 g (2¼ oz) plain flour
pinch of salt
2 caramel chocolate eggs, each split in half

**1.** Melt the chocolate and butter in the microwave, stir to combine, then leave to cool for 10 minutes.

**2.** Preheat the air fryer to 160°C/325°F. Butter 4 ramekins (about 8 cm/3¼ inch in diameter).

**3.** Beat the eggs into the chocolate mix one at a time, then fold through the sugar, flour and salt until fully combined.

**4.** Divide the mixture between the prepared ramekins. Use the back of a spoon to flatten the top of the mixture, then push half a caramel egg into each pot.

**5.** Place the ramekins into the air fryer drawer, then cook for 15 minutes. Leave to stand for a couple of minutes before enjoying.

**Tip**

If you like salted caramel, sprinkle a few sea salt flakes on top before cooking.

20 MINS

 18 MINS

 VEGETARIAN

*I had to find an inventive way to use my favourite chocolate bar in my air fryer, so I created these moreish cookies that are perfect for a sweet treat. I love the way they are both crispy and chewy at the same time, as a good cookie should be. I use an ice cream scoop to ball up the dough and create perfectly uniform biscuits every time.*

# DAIM BAR CHOCOLATE COOKIES

**MAKES 10**

---

125 g (4½ oz) unsalted butter, melted
180 g (6 oz) golden caster sugar
1 egg
225 g (8 oz) plain flour
½ teaspoon bicarbonate of soda
2 Daim bars, crushed into small shards

**1.** In a bowl with an electric whisk, or in a food mixer fitted with the whisk attachment, cream together the butter and sugar, then beat in the egg until fully incorporated. Sift in the flour and bicarbonate of soda, toss in most of the Daim bar shards (reserve some for sprinkling on top), then fold until fully combined. Use an ice cream scoop to portion the cookie dough into 10 cookies, about 60 g (2¼ oz) each.

---

**2.** Preheat the air fryer to 160°C/325°F.

---

**3.** Place the dough balls on the crisp plate inside the air fryer drawer, flatten them slightly, then top with the remaining Daim bar shards. Bake the cookies for 18 minutes, then remove and cool on a wire rack. (You may need to do this in batches, depending on the size of your air fryer.)

---

**Tip**

If you want perfectly round cookies, as soon as they come out of the air fryer, pop them on a work surface, then swirl them under a large glass to shape them back into rounds. It doesn't matter if you don't, though, as they still taste great.

# INDEX

# UK–US GLOSSARY

Aubergines – eggplants
Bacon rashers – bacon slices
Baking paper – parchment paper
Banging – amazing/brilliant/fantastic
Bicarbonate of soda – baking soda
Biscoff spread – speculoos cookie butter
Biscuits – cookies
Black treacle – blackstrap molasses
Caster sugar – superfine sugar
Chestnut mushrooms – cremini mushrooms
Chips – fries
Cider vinegar – apple cider vinegar
Clingfilm – plastic wrap
Coriander leaves – cilantro leaves
Cornflour – corn starch
Courgette – zucchini
Crisps – chips
Desiccated coconut – unsweetened
    shredded coconut
Double cream – heavy cream
Faff – fuss
Golden caster sugar – unrefined
    superfine sugar

Grated – shredded
Green pepper/red pepper –
    green/red bell pepper
King prawns – jumbo shrimp
Lush – delicious
Maris Piper potatoes –
    all-rounder potatoes
Mature cheese – sharp cheese
Mexicana cheese – cheese with added
    bell peppers, garlic salt and chilli;
    Pepper Jack may be substituted
Minced meat – ground meat
Muffins – English muffins
Peckishness – hunger
Plain flour – all-purpose flour
Prawns – shrimp
Rolled oats – old-fashioned oats
Scones – biscuits
Self-raising flour – self-rising flour
Stitched-up – cheated
Streaky bacon – bacon
Toastie/toasted sandwich –
    grilled cheese

# THANK YOU

Sometimes in life, I just have to pinch myself to make sure this is all really happening. Those days all those years ago, when I was sat on my digger in my construction job, dreaming about what I was going to make for dinner that evening, seem a lifetime away. I truly can't believe some of the opportunities that have been given to me over the years since I first got into the world of food back in 2006 after *MasterChef*.

Becoming a cookbook author for me was an absolute pipe dream and I still cannot believe I am the author of five, soon to be six, cookbooks. When I first started out, the thought of having a singular book with my name and cheesy grin on the front cover was something I truly thought would've been out of my reach, so I feel so lucky. Of course, these opportunities wouldn't have arrived without the love, help and support of all the people around me who have made this book possible. I want to thank you all but need also to mention a special few.

My amazing wife, Liz, your support for me in everything I do means the world to me. You're always there for me to lend an ear and bounce ideas off, I must bore you to tears, but you never complain. Where would I be without my chief taster? I could tell you that I'd be absolutely nowhere. I love you more than you'll ever know.

My little superstar, Indie. I cannot even begin to tell you how proud you make all of us. You are the perfect role model to your beautiful little sister, Vivvy, who is growing up just like you – although she does have better banter. Keep following your dreams and working hard. I couldn't wish for a better daughter and you will always be my biggest inspiration.

I have a huge and amazing family. Not only do I have amazing parents in Dad, Lynn, Mum and Paul, but also now Vicky and Glenn too. Your support and encouragement mean I can keep pursuing my dream. And my memories of growing up in a foodie family have truly inspired me to push to get where I am today.

To Borra, Jan, Louise, Megan, Viera and the rest of the team at DML Talent, I'll always be grateful to you for the continuing opportunities that mean I can chase my dream of working in the world of food.

To everyone at Octopus publishing, thank you so much for the continued support and opportunities to write and publish my recipes in your books. Getting my food out there for people to cook at home has always been my biggest passion and driving force and you've given me this amazing opportunity on four occasions. Huge thank you to Polly, Natalie, Jaz, Lucy and the rest of the team.

Emma and Alex at Smith & Gilmour, it was amazing to have the opportunity to work with you again. Thank you for being patient and listening to me in regards to how I wanted the book to turn out. You are legends.

Tom, Agathe, Troy, Arnaud and Jess for bringing my food to life, not an easy task with such a niche subject, but the images far surpassed anything I thought possible. I massively appreciate all of the long hours and the hard work you put in to this book. It's nothing short of spectacular.

Finally, thank you to everyone who has supported me through my cooking journey over the last few years. Social media has become a huge part of my work life and to all those supporters who have taken the time to follow me, engage with my content, message me, share pics of your cooking with me and offer me words of encouragement, I'm nothing without you. Oh, and Jonny Gwyves, make sure you order your usual 50 copies of this book as always.

# ABOUT THE AUTHOR

Dean Edwards made his first TV appearance on BBC's *MasterChef Goes Large* in 2006, an experience that inspired him to pursue a career in food. Since then, he has been a regular on such UK TV shows as ITV's *Lorraine* and *This Morning*, and has amassed a strong community of more than 777,000 across his social media platforms, where he posts fuss-free recipes for everyday eating. Dean's ethos is that food should be achievable, simple and, above all, taste fantastic, with ingredients that are inexpensive and accessible.

@deanedwardschef

hamlyn

First published in Great Britain in 2023 by Hamlyn,
an imprint of Octopus Publishing Group Ltd
Carmelite House
50 Victoria Embankment
London EC4Y 0DZ
www.octopusbooks.co.uk

An Hachette UK Company
www.hachette.co.uk

Text copyright © Dean Edwards 2023
Design and layout copyright © Octopus Publishing Group 2023

Distributed in the US by Hachette Book Group, 1290 Avenue
of the Americas, 4th and 5th Floors, New York, NY 10104

Distributed in Canada by Canadian Manda Group,
664 Annette St, Toronto, Ontario, Canada M6S 2C8

ISBN 978-0-60063-798-1

A CIP catalogue record for this book is available from the British Library.

Printed and bound in China.

10 9 8 7 6 5 4 3 2 1

Editorial Director: Natalie Bradley
Senior Editor: Pollyanna Poulter
Copy Editor: Lucy Bannell
Art Director: Jaz Bahra
Design and Art Direction: Smith & Gilmour
Photographer: Tom Regester
Food Stylist: Troy Willis
Prop Stylist: Agathe Gits
Production Manager: Caroline Alberti